God Recycles Broken Dreams

An Intimate Look at my Down-to-Earth Heavenly Father's Care

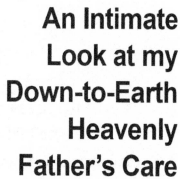

Ruth Shank Shira

ANM
publishers

God Recycles Broken Dreams

Published by:

Advancing Native Missions
P.O. Box 5303 ✦ Charlottesville, VA 22905
www.AdvancingNativeMissions.com

Cover & Interior Design: *Heather Kirk, GraphicsForSuccess.com*

Acknowledgments

I am deeply indebted to Advancing Native Missions' ANM PRESS for giving me the opportunity to share my life's story with you.

I thank my family and friends, who have generously allowed me to use their names in describing particular incidents and phases of my life's journey. They lend authenticity to my God story.

Special gratitude goes to my daughter, Beverly Sue Shank. Not only was she my cherished child during some very intense struggles, she became my closest friend as she grew into adulthood.

Thank you goes to Sue Morris for the hours and hours of transferring, word by word, my antiquated typing into a modern computer-based word processing format.

Getting this book into your hands, and hopefully your heart, would not have been possible without the editing efforts of Brenda Thacker and Virginia Tobias. Your suggestions and gentle words of advice were very helpful.

A big thank you, too, to Heather Kirk of *Graphics For Success* for a creative and beautifully designed cover and layout.

To all these and anyone I may have inadvertently overlooked, I will always remain grateful and appreciative for your encouragement and moral support to complete my story, which God himself wrote years before I was even born.

Dedication

To my priceless heritage, including not only my godly parents but also the many pastors, Sunday school teachers, and missionaries, together with countless saints of God who both taught me about him and exemplified the life of the Lord Jesus Christ, I dedicate this story of his life in me.

All have inspired me throughout my childhood and youth and impacted me for eternity.

I concur with the Psalmist David, "The godly people in the land are my true heroes! I take pleasure in them" (Psalm 16:3).

Prologue

To many, life seems like a never-ending parade of problems! The distraught housewife, coping with the exhausting demands of husband and children, community involvement and often an outside job, cries out in despair, "Will someone please stop this hectic merry-go-round? I need to get off and rest awhile!" Or even more frustrating is the role of the single parent, who sighs heavily, "How can I ever handle all these added responsibilities while coping with my state of loneliness?" The pressured businessman calculates apprehensively how much longer he can survive the cut-throat competition in this cold computerized world. Insecure children and bewildered teenagers wonder, "What's there to live for? No one even cares about me."

Piercing this cloud of fatalistic gloom are the undaunted church spires pointing us heavenward. Robed choirs sing their anthems of praise, and staid clergymen proclaim, "Come our way—we have the answers to your problems!" But do they really? Why are there so many empty church pews? Why do so many worshippers come out appearing as burdened as when they entered? And why do hundreds of disillusioned clergymen hang up their clerical robes in pursuit of fulfillment?

These are some of the questions that I will address in the following pages, for I too was forced by the hard hand of bitter experience to bridge this chasm from *Sunday's glory* to *Monday's mourning*. When my long-awaited baby was born, the doctor announced in subdued tones, "He's a boy, but something went wrong ... your baby is not alive." My soul cried out in agony, "God, where *are* you!" Then there have been those almost daily stresses such as when my loaded washing machine came to a grinding halt. Or when there were insufficient funds in the bank for taxes or medical care. Or when my ten-year-old car had already gone beyond the mileage of duty, and the mechanic said quite candidly, "I'm not going to charge you for this repair because I can't guarantee it will hold together long enough to get out of my garage." And indeed it didn't! Theological dogmas, denominational doctrines or religious clichés were meaningless to me. My hurting soul searched for a *down-to-earth God!*

But the most traumatic test of all came as my lifelong dream of being a minister's wife was destroyed, and I found myself in a divorce court facing disbelief and despair. In that dark abyss of soul-searching and sleepless nights that followed, I was painfully stripped, layer by layer, of idealism, pious platitudes, and traditional bondages. As my naked, aching soul plummeted to the ground, I cried out in almost accusing agony, "Now where are you, God?" And in loving, shockingly simple assurance he replied, "I'm right here where you landed—*down-to-earth.* I've been here all the time. In fact, my Son arrived here two thousand years ago so he could show you the way."

Then I reflected upon how Jesus Christ, the Son of God, was born into humble circumstances and likely hammered nails in Joseph's carpenter shop. Then as the itinerant Teacher, he walked dusty roads and through bending wheat fields, taking time to bless the little children, to comment on the birds and animals, and to bring joy at a wedding celebration. He gave life and hope to the sick and sorrowing along his way. Yes, he, too, became hungry, thirsty, weary and lonely. He was misunderstood, falsely accused, and ultimately crucified. I would have to admit that Jesus Christ was very much down-to-earth!

So, humbly and gratefully, I followed. Here's my story of that down-to-earth walk with the Son of Man. And as I share how he has been walking along life's road with me, may you take courage to realize that he desires to walk with you on your journey, too.

Table of Contents

> I discovered new meaning in the Easter message during my
> stressful divorce proceedings on the Monday following Easter.

> Disclosing my hurt, anger and frustration as a result of smashed
> dreams and goals, I learned many invaluable lessons in this
> wilderness experience.

> After my respectable roles disintegrated, I suffered humiliation as
> just a Fill-in, but God taught me through the ordinary egg how
> important I truly was!

> I learned not only to make the best of an undesirable state of
> affairs, but how to actually enjoy it, accepting all the benefits...
> including a 25th wedding anniversary trip to Hawaii—alone!

God Recycles **Broken** *Dreams*

Chapter 1
Monday Mourning

It was Easter Sunday 1973, and the minister's lovely wife was singing in her beautiful, ascending tones, "Because he lives I can face tomorrow; because he lives all fear is gone; because I know, I know who holds the future, and life is worth the living just because he lives." Sitting alone in the rear of that large sanctuary, all that my sobbing heart could hear were the words from Bill Gaither's song, "Because he lives, I can face tomorrow..."

"Tomorrow"... my tomorrow meant that dreaded day when I would appear in the county Superior Court of California to proceed with the dissolution of my twenty-three year marriage. And to add "insult to injury," because of financial necessity, this whole painful process was being handled in accordance with the Do-Your-Own-Divorce plan.

"Oh, God, how can I face tomorrow? I feel so alone and hurt so deeply. Can this really be happening to me? All my dreams are shattered and my comfortable roles and goals are gone. What will people say? How can I face tomorrow?"

To appear before the judge *in pro per*, without an attorney, seemed frightening! All those legal terms—*petition, proof of service, interlocutory judgment, final judgment*—all these were dreadfully awesome. Had the California courts adopted the term "dissolution" to cushion this painful trauma? But how can feelings, experiences and memories of twenty-three years ever be dissolved? On the other hand, to use the word "divorce," although it more realistically described the broken heart, seemed unspeakable with all the stigma and shame it carried. It just did not have a place in the vocabulary of either my family or my husband's.

While the minister's wife was still singing, and with the worshippers dressed in their Easter finery, I found myself viewing a flashback of the past several years. I recalled that dreary day in November 1969 while living in the state of Maine. It was with heavy heart and trudging footsteps that he was carrying his personal belongings from our house to his Chevy station wagon. In that emotion-packed moment of final farewell to his weeping wife and bewildered eight-year-old daughter, my husband, Lloyd, was unable to say more than just mutter, "I must go to New York City." Disenchanted, disillusioned and unfulfilled with life and position, he felt he needed to escape in search of a new life.

"It can't be… it's not true, God… that's my husband with whom I've shared intimately the joys and sorrows of life for nineteen years!"

"In our pastorates in New York, Pennsylvania, Florida, and Maine, he has been a patient, kind shepherd to many of your flock. He has counseled others in distress. His dedication to you was often remarkable. Oh, God, please let this be just a bad dream that will vanish by morning!"

But he did not return. Sleepless nights. Soul searching. Agonizing prayers. Fountains of tears.

"Friends and relatives, where are you? You comforted me in the untimely death of my father and of my infant son, but somehow, now, you don't understand. Please don't talk about him … that only intensifies my pain."

"God, my whole world has collapsed! Since I was a very young child, you know the secret between you and me of my wanting to be a minister's wife, but now that dream is utterly shattered. And since I had such a secure home as a child, I took it for granted that my daughter would have the same. What will her friends think and say now? How can I protect her? God, are you there? I feel like I'm being dashed against the rocks by merciless waves of sorrow."

Then I saw on the screen of my memory his periodic return visits with all the emotional stress of such an estranged arrangement. Finally, in response to my plea for a together family again, he suggested we, our ten-year-old daughter and I, move to New Jersey in the environs of New York City. It was a grueling ordeal to try to find an apartment for less than three hundred dollars a month, and even the one we did rent was infested with crawling creatures that seemed to resent our taking over. Beverly, our daughter, had to face the added strain of being thrust into a school situation which was heaving with racial problems. And I, bereft of friends and relatives in this new location, all against the backdrop of a foreboding marital horizon, was being depleted of mental and emotional resources.

In the midst of this exhausting experience, my dear sister Esther called from California. "Ruthie, you just can't go on like this! Why don't you and Bev come out to our place and stay with us for awhile? We'd be so glad to have you."

And my kind-hearted brother-in-law, with his ever-ready MasterCard, proceeded to make plane reservations for us for the following Saturday.

I remembered how on the evening before our supposed departure, being restless and unable to sleep, I had slipped out of bed and tiptoed downstairs with my Bible. And there in the Book of Ruth (of all Books!) these words seemed to leap out in bold print: "Sit still, my daughter, until thou knows how the matter will fall…" (Ruth 3:18). That was God telling me to sit it out a little longer and not to move ahead of his perfect timing.

Then I recalled how in desperation I sought out a very fine minister and counselor, who had been trained in the family counseling services of the Marble Collegiate Church in New York City. He was truly a partial fulfillment of Isaiah's prophecy that Jesus Christ would be "Wonderful, Counselor…" (Isaiah 9:6), for the Christ-like life within Rev. Callaway understood my grief, frustration and fears. He handled my self-doubt delicately but with positive direction. When I shared woefully, "If only I didn't feel so deeply about him and everything involved, I wouldn't hurt so much," Mr. Callaway replied comfortingly, "But because you are that kind of person, you have a large capacity for life."

Distressing dreams of painful dental extractions, of a mother cat carrying away her dead kittens one by one, of almost drowning while trying to rescue some possessions—all these Mr. Callaway helped to identify as a deep inner turmoil over the loss of much that had been very precious to me—a husband, our home, my aspirations for the future. Then he would skillfully lead me to face reality. He would repeatedly urge, "Ruth, you must let the anger and hurt surface and face them." At first, I found this to be almost devastating, but as I released all those confusing feelings to God, I would experience a deep, cleansing relief.

Christmas of '71 came into full focus on this rolling film. For Beverly's sake (my 10-year-old daughter) I had tried to bolster my drooping spirit enough to decorate our apartment with a small Christmas tree, candles on the mantle and a log in the fireplace. But there really was no glow in our sad hearts. Mr. Callaway had reminded me, "Ruth, this may not be a happy Christmas for you, but it can be a meaningful one."

And that it was. I identified in deeper dimensions than ever before with the humiliation, anxieties, and frustrations of Mary, Joseph, the shepherds, the innkeeper and others of that first Christmas. The Word was truly becoming flesh through my own experiences. Also, the phrase, "in the fullness of time" seemed to take on new meaning. As in Christ's earthly life there were stages, so too there were stages in my life. Each stage had to reach its fullness before the next step in God's plan could be realized.

Eating our Christmas dinner in a festively decorated restaurant with singing waiters and waitresses should have inspired some holiday feelings, but the joyful sounds and twinkling lights seemed to mock this lonely-hearted threesome. Traditionally, we had always enjoyed our annual Christmas evening ride around town to see all the brightly decorated homes, but after viewing just a few, I said rather sadly, "Please let's go back to the apartment." How can one see glittering lights through a veil of sorrow!

There were some rather strange but meaningful happenings during that season. With some difficulty I had selected a subdued plaid sport shirt for my husband as a Christmas gift. I was almost stunned as I watched the clerk choose a gold colored box and a black bow with which to wrap this gift. Somehow the black bow symbolized my mourning over the "death" of our relationship (and I do believe emotional or spiritual death is more agonizingly painful than physical death). And the golden box represented the refining process that my

God Recycles **Broken** *Dreams*

faith and inner nature were going through. Signing the gift tag was almost impossible; intimate pet names faded into distant memory in my detached, ambivalent state of mind.

Several days after that bleak Christmas, my estranged husband said, "Pal, we can't go on like this. I believe I'll move back to my room in the city." The inevitable was a sad relief.

In the Christmas mail there was another gracious invitation from Esther and her husband, Wayne. Esther quoted I Cor. 10:13, "There hath no temptation taken you but such as is common to man: but God is faithful, who will not allow you to be tempted above that you are able; but will with the temptation also make a way to escape, that you may be able to bear it," and suggested, "I feel God could use us to be that 'escape' out of this situation."

Previously, I had not sensed God's release, but now there was nothing to hold Beverly and me any longer in this undesirable location.

To hasten our decision to move to California, there came a call informing me that my mother, who also lived there, had suffered a heart attack. Various scriptures in my daily devotional time also seemed to point to this change: "Arise, and depart, for this is not your rest: because it is polluted, it shall destroy you, even with a sore destruction" (Mt. 2:10). These divine words confirmed Mr. Callaway's counsel, "This area is not the place for you and Bev. There's no future here for you."

Beverly, in her young but perceptive way, said, "I feel like I've been put through a time machine and am living in the future. That's why I haven't been able to get real close to kids at school—this is their home but not mine. I'm just passing through. This isn't our home really. I feel like we made the wrong turn, and we need someone to help us get on the main path again. Life shouldn't be so much sadness!"

Well, there was Someone to lead us on the right paths. And he reassured me with such promises as: "In all their afflictions he was afflicted, and the Angel of his presence saved them; in his love and in his pity he redeemed them; and bore them all the days of old" (Isa. 63:9). "For this God is our God forever and ever; he will be our guide even unto death" (Ps. 48:14). "Thine eyes shall see the king in his beauty: and they shall behold the land that is very far off" (Isaiah 33:17). "As an eagle stirreth up her nest, fluttereth over her young, spreadeth abroad her wings, taketh them, beareth them on her wings: so the Lord alone did lead him..." (Deut. 32:11-12). And if it were true that "... hitherto hath the Lord helped us" (I Sam. 7:12), in no way would he forsake us now!

But even with all these sure promises to strengthen my fearful heart, my soul was still struggling with battered emotions and a deflated ego. How could I ever forget that evening as I was sorting and packing our belongings in preparation for the trek across country! Somehow when I got to that very special box, so sentimentally preserved, containing my satin wedding gown, together with my treasured album of love letters, pressed roses with satin bow—memoirs of our once-blooming romance—the sight and memories of all these were more than I could handle. It seemed as if a mighty Niagara Falls burst forth in torrents of tears. Very deliberately, I piled all these emotion-packed items into my arms, and with angry steps carried them outside and stashed them in the cold trash cans. Just as I came back in, the phone rang—what timing! My sister-in-law, Grace, was calling from Wisconsin, and in her loving voice was inquiring, "Ruthie, Marv and I are just wondering how you're doing."

Sobbingly, I blurted out, "I just threw away my wedding gown, love letters, diaries—it's all over!"

Her soothing remarks were like an assuring embrace from God, "Please know that we love you and that we're praying for you." "Oh thank you, God. You must still care."

And truly he does care, and in such detailed ways. For in that very same week of packing, an ad appeared in the newspaper: "Moving to San Francisco, will move your furniture on shared-expense basis."

This proved to be a very economical way to get our household goods to California and just within the right area. "Thank you, Father."

Those last few days spent in New Jersey were filled with many tokens of God's love and direction. My last session with Mr. Callaway proved helpful

God Recycles **Broken** *Dreams*

in months to come. He said, "I want to protect you for the future. You have to think in terms of functioning in a new framework, no longer in the role of a minister's wife. Don't focus on the past with its hurtful scenes—that's only daydreaming—focus on a new life and a new role. I envision you either in Christian education or as being ordained as a minister. It probably will take one to two years for your injured feelings to heal and to know just where you are going, but with your perceptive nature, you will know. Make changes just a step at a time and be sure to absorb changes before taking the next step. I think you need to face up to the possibility of divorce. Your husband has taken on an entirely different lifestyle that is completely incompatible with yours."

"But what about Jesus' teaching on divorce," I asked tearfully.

"Jesus was never a legalist," he replied. "The ideal is to have two live together inseparably, but how many are able! To live in distress and anguish is against the very Spirit of Christ."

There were kind farewells from the export office crew at Faberge' where I had worked for several months. To brighten up Beverly's trip, I had purchased an attractive red travel alarm clock and a cute Valentine doll which dangled from our visor.

Friends and relatives had expressed concern over my driving those 3,300 miles "alone," especially since winter still had its grip on much of the area to be traveled. California did seem terribly far away, but when I thought in terms of just four hundred miles a day, it did not seem quite as fearsome. Dr. Robert Schuller says, "Inch by inch, life's a cinch; by the yard, life is hard!" But what really gave me courage for the venture was the scripture made alive to me the very morning of our departure: "Jesus himself drew near, and went with them..." (Luke 24:15 KJV). In such good company we were safe!

And truly he was with us from the very start—even if in a rather frustrating way. Our '65 Skylark Buick was all packed up and ready to go, but it would not go! The local garage man discovered a broken hose, a leaky gas line and a choke in need of repair. This delay was really a blessing in disguise. Once on the highway, we encountered snow and slush only in Pennsylvania; after that, it was as if God had opened another Red Sea and let us go through on dry ground over areas where there had been severe ice and snow storms just days previous to our being there.

God's protective guidance became clear when we discovered near Indianapolis, Indiana that we had a rather serious radiator leak. I "happened" to pull off the turnpike at a garage where the mechanic had a successful record of repairing race car radiators. "If this stuff doesn't take care of your problem—nothing will," he declared. It worked fine!

As we traveled through wintry scenes, the starkly naked trees, stripped of all their foliage by the cold, relentless winds, spoke to me in mute testimony and encouragement: "You, too, can come through this storm standing up, even though you are stripped of so much that mattered."

After seven days and 3,300 miles, with friends in the East pushing and relatives in the West pulling, Beverly and I arrived safely at Esther and Wayne's home on February 19, 1972. When they heard the honking of our car horn, they rushed outside with open hearts and home. Loving nieces—Valerie, Karen and Lynette—had rearranged sleeping quarters to accommodate their cousin and aunt. This was to be our "haven of rest" for the next six months.

Oh… yes, here I am… back again… the minister's wife is still singing, "Because he lives, I can face tomorrow…" I'm glad there's no one sitting right next to me, for all those memories have opened fountains of tears… I hope no one is looking my way.

But someone does seem very close… Thank you for sitting down next to me, Lord. And since you are so near may I whisper to you how I feel? All this celebration about Easter—new life, spring flowers, happy songs—they all seem so far away from where I am. In fact, they actually seem to mock my sorrowful heart. I feel like I'm driving in the rain at night with my blurry vision.

Then, without a hint of rebuke in his voice, Jesus Christ reminded me, "Don't you remember broken-hearted Mary Magdalene, who came to my tomb that first Easter? Also blinded by sorrow, she wept because my tomb was empty. She should have wept if it had *not* been empty. She, too, felt that all her

God Recycles **Broken** *Dreams*

hopes and dreams were now buried in a cold, dark tomb. But all this time she was just on the outside looking in—a rather limited perspective you would have to agree. Because of her grief, she even failed to recognize me in the midst, mistaking me for the gardener, and even blaming me for having taken her Lord away. In the exaggerated emotions of the moment, she even offered to care for my body—all quite unrealistic" (John 20:1-18 KJV).

"Well then, Lord, how did you handle all this?"

"I simply spoke her name... 'Mary'... and in an instant of illumination she knew I was her living Lord. And so, 'Ruth'..."

"Oh, Jesus, I know you are with me, I know you are alive, and because you are, I know I can face tomorrow! My Lord and my Master!"

Chapter 2
A Letter to God

El Sobrante, California
May 21, 1972

Dear God,

I'm mad and terribly frustrated and confused!

You know that I have loved and tried to honor and serve you from my childhood. You promised if I'd seek first your kingdom, all else would be added (Matt. 6:33 KJV); it looks more like all else has been subtracted—my husband, home, identity, career, and material possessions.

I've always loved your Word and have been illuminated repeatedly by the Holy Spirit with inspirations. But with whom do I share? All doors seem to be closed. I'm so frustrated by it all!

You promised if I'd acknowledge you in all my ways, you would direct me. I do thank you for guidance many times, but where do I go from here? Please show me the way! Open your door! You promised if I'd ask anything in the name of Jesus and for your glory, you would do it. I expect an answer this week in some direction—on the basis of your Word—for my sake and yours. Thank you.

Expectantly,
Your child

Although by the next morning I had humbly added a postscript on the above letter asking forgiveness for my impudent grievance and command, yet this letter conveyed in limited measure the indescribable anguish I was experiencing. I felt like a misplaced person in a state of numb suspension between a "has-been" and a "what-will-I-become?" This whole tragedy was an unplanned, unwanted, and undeserved interruption in my life.

And this break had not been a sudden catastrophe, but rather the culmination of about ten years of stressing and grieving over the erratic paths my husband was taking. Sleepless nights, humiliations, anxious hours—all these had taken their toll. Such continuous trauma registered in my body in the form of hypoglycemia, with its accompanying symptoms of weakness and blackouts. In this state of emotional depletion I experienced nagging self-doubts and exaggerated anxiety at times and even a sense of hopelessness. It seemed as though I were groping along in a dark, endless tunnel. Yet somehow etched upon the walls of this dismal tunnel, I would catch glimpses of inscriptions such as, "Your days of mourning all will end" (Isaiah 60:20) and "Weeping may go on all night, but in the morning there is joy" (Psalm 30:5).

Oh, God, will morning ever come?

In the midst of this dark valley, those two devastating monsters—Resentment and Self-pity—would rise up repeatedly and attempt to solicit my attention with such patronizing words as, *what did you ever do to deserve this?* Moments of indulgence with these gray ghosts would only cause the shroud of gloom to grow heavier. To loosen their death-like grip, the faithful Holy Spirit would inspire me repeatedly to "offer the sacrifice of thanksgiving" (Psalm 116:17) to God for his presence and power in the midst of the problem. Praise at a time like this truly was a sacrifice, but it always gave me a rewarding sense of peace and assurance that God was in control.

My sorrow seemed to take me through stages. First, there was the initial shock of loss—perhaps akin to the feeling experienced by those suddenly bereft of all earthly possessions by fire or flood. But my loss was the severance of an intimate relationship, probably even more painful than a physical loss

God Recycles **Broken** *Dreams*

since it was in the spiritual and emotional realms. In this stage, I had difficulty comprehending that this was actually happening to me. I had heard about marital breakups of neighbors and acquaintances. I had read the cold statistics in magazine articles, but now I was one of them. *Perhaps this will be a temporary separation,* I would console myself. However, the uncertainty of it all only added to the stress of my present state.

From that painful initial shock, I descended into a valley of deep sorrow. At first it was a prolonged sorrow for what seemed to be a waste of the potentially valuable life of my ex-minister husband. I wept until I felt I could weep no more. I spent many hours in intercessory prayer and fasting on his behalf, claiming Isaiah 57:18 KJV, "I have seen his ways, and will heal him: I will lead him also, and restore comforts unto him and to his mourners."

Finally, in desperation, I released my husband to God with these words, "Lord, he belonged to you before I ever knew him, and he will be in your hands long after I'm gone, so just take full charge of him now." There is a great relief in just giving up. "Give your burdens to the Lord. He will carry them" (Psalm 55:22).

The focus of grief then shifted from him to my own needs. He said he had to leave the church and our home and marriage in order to find himself, a new lifestyle with self-fulfillment. So this gave me a feeling of rejection, wondering *what's wrong with me?* All my life I had experienced warm acceptance by friends and family. Now suddenly I'm rejected—a painful, humbling experience.

In this valley of humiliation there are so many glaring lights and pointing fingers to accentuate one's stripped single state of affairs—job application forms, medical forms, tax forms all force a person to check one's marital status. Oh, God, why must there be so many poignant reminders of my agony in being a divorcee!

Being single, I felt like a social cripple, a fifth wheel in the vehicle of a couples' gathering, and to attend a "singles' social" seemed to underline my new dilemma in even bolder uncertainties. Thank God for emotionally mature couples who can reach out and embrace a hurting single without treating her as a threat to their own security. Attending a wedding or an anniversary celebration magnified my pain because of my shattered ideals and dreams. Just as Jesus himself suffered the most unexpected abuse from the religious folk of his day, so many "Pharisaical Christians" (if there can really be such a breed!) find it easier to condemn and restrict the hurting single than to minister the healing graces of our Savior. But again, praise God for the true followers of Jesus Christ who show compassion and minister the grace of acceptance to the broken-hearted.

All these day-by-day circumstances reinforced the humiliating process until the valley of humiliation led to an even deeper depression. *Will this ever change? What are all our friends and relatives saying? How can I ever feel normal again?*

These questions haunted me day and night, and added to my sense of failure and rejection with the choking clutches of loneliness and insecurity. With my role as minister's wife broken, what do I do now? With whom do I share all those daily stresses and joys?

Finally, I approached the edge of reality. Falteringly and painfully, I had to accept the fact of where I was, and instead of disintegrating into a useless nobody, I had to take steps to be rehabilitated by God's grace into a useful somebody. Encouraged by his voice, "The Lord is close to those whose hearts are breaking" (Psalm 34:18), I started thinking in terms of reconstructing my torn-down life structure. "Forgetting the past and looking forward to what lies ahead…" (Philippians 3:13), I was strengthened to go on. Using God's Word makes for such strong building material! When longing for the secure roles of the past, God would say, "But forget all that—it is nothing compared to what I'm going to do, for I'm going to do a brand new thing. See, I have already begun! Don't you see it? I will make a road through the wilderness for my people to go home, and create rivers for them in the desert" (Isaiah 43:18-19).

Before I could lay a firm foundation for a new life, I felt the need for a deep inner cleansing and healing of all my former hurts—like clearing away the debris of a wrecked building having to be cleared away before a new one could be built on that same site. Or perhaps I could be likened to a tooth needing to be drilled and cleaned before the repair.

God Recycles **Broken** *Dreams*

The most effective healing balm for the wounded spirit is *love*. Just to be able to rest in Esther's and Wayne's home and to know Beverly was safe in a healthy, happy household with bouncy cousins was a comfort to me. There are fragile moments when love needs no words; just its very presence conveys tenderly and assuringly the message, *I care*. Often Esther and Wayne would sit quietly and compassionately by my bedside as the tears flowed uncontrollably. And dear Mother, who lived right next door, would come into the room with a freshly picked rose from her rose garden, saying, "Here, Ruthie, look at this pretty one."

Even Rex, the family Sheltie, seemed to sense he had a special duty to stay near me with his protective companionship.

Friends and neighbors would stop by or drop a note in the mail assuring me of their concern and God's care. One day when I was in the depths of despair, the phone rang; it was Rebecca Gilkey, a dear friend and saint from Florida whom I had not seen for about ten years. She said, "God just dropped you into my heart this morning while I was reading his Word, and I don't really know what you are going through right now, but everything is going to be alright— just rest in the Lord."

"Lord, you must really love me and care for me to prompt someone way across the country to call and assure me of your concern. Thank you, Father."

God not only communicates to us through his children, but also through nature. I found taking walks was therapeutic—especially since it was springtime, with its gorgeous array of bright yellow acacia trees and pink Japanese plum tree blossoms. All nature seemed to proclaim: *there is new life and beauty—just look at us!*

Not only is love a sure cure for the sorrowful spirit, but so too is time. Time, used by the skillful hands of the divine Physician, does wonders, for he knows just when to bring the right circumstance, the right book or the right person into our lives. God did just that for me by sending his anointed servant, J. B. Oaks, from Oklahoma, to minister in a nearby California church. What was originally scheduled as a regular five-evening teaching seminar was extended for three weeks. God's timepiece chimed the time for that performance! It would be a selfish interpretation to think that God extended the meeting just for me, but it is comforting to realize that his love for us is limitless.

Every evening for those three weeks, the theme of Oaks' beautiful ministry was, "Let God turn your bruises into blessings and your wounds into wealth." (His message was especially effective because he and his wife were going through a valley of sorrow from the loss of their infant.)

Each evening, at the conclusion of his life-giving words, the congregation would sit in quiet worship and meditation as Jesus seemed to tiptoe among us freely dispensing his healing grace and love. He would whisper as he passed by, "I heal the broken-hearted, binding up their wounds" (Psalm 147:3). "I, even I, am he that comforteth you..." (Isaiah 51:12 KJV).

In the midst of this purifying healing experience, God gave me this song:

> In his presence, all strivings cease,
>
> In his presence, there's sweet release;
>
> In his presence—such joy and peace!
>
> Oh hallowed presence, in him complete.

Throughout this prolonged spiritual healing session there were recurrences of distress and anxiety, but with declining intensity. I found relief as I would withdraw into quiet communion in his presence—not in a regimented Bible reading time or a legalistic church attendance—but in a restful quietness in his presence, allowing him to restore my soul. The assimilation of one's grief is necessary, and this cannot be obtained in the noisy, bustling crowd. Even Jesus felt the need to withdraw into the wilderness after having received the shocking news of his cousin's cruel death at the hands of the drunken Herod: "As soon as Jesus heard the news, he went off by himself in a boat to a remote area to be alone" (Matthew 14:13).

So as part of God's reconstruction plan for my life, there was that wilderness experience. This was the stage where I felt like a nobody going nowhere.

In this barren wasteland, life seemed meaningless and unproductive. It was an uncharted path without route signs—what a distressing dilemma! "Lord, I've trained for your work, have served you faithfully... why now this vast vacuum?"

As my spirit would agonizingly question God, "Please show me what I can do for you," invariably his reply would be, "Don't worry so much about what you can do for me, but rather what I am trying to do in you; *being* is so much more important than *doing*."

That would remind me of the wise exhortation of a veteran missionary saint I had met in the early years of our pastoral work. Although physically blind, she had keen insight into the purposes of God. "Ruth," she had shared, "Whenever God gave me an assignment, it wasn't so much what I accomplished for him that mattered, but rather what he worked within me that was important."

This seemed to be the experience of the Israelites as they were wandering in their wilderness, "...the Lord led you through the wilderness for all these forty years, humbling you and testing you to find out how you would respond, and whether or not you would really obey him" (Deut. 8:2). Not only was this true of the Israelites but also any of God's servants, past and present, who have had their wilderness experiences.

Joseph, in spite of his dreams and aspirations, was set aside in a prison for thirteen years by seemingly unfair circumstances. "There in prison they hurt his feet with fetters and placed his neck in an iron collar until God's time finally came—how God tested his patience" (Psalm 105:18).

Moses, highly trained for leadership in the lavish courts of Egypt, had to be taken aside into God's wilderness university for forty years before he was prepared to be a humble and effective leader for the next forty years.

David, although the chosen and anointed king of Israel, spent years fleeing and hiding in one cave after another in the wilderness until he inherited his God-ordained throne.

The Holy Spirit led Paul into the Arabian Desert for several years to assimilate his drastic conversion and prepare for the effective sharing of his testimony.

Even Jesus Christ was tempted for forty days in the wilderness before the onset of his public ministry.

So it seems that my wilderness experience was needful for my spiritual growth—a period of refining my devotion to God and redefining his purpose for my life. "I refined you in the furnace of affliction" (Isaiah 48:10).

But how comforting to realize that the same God who had "... led forth his own people like a flock, guiding them safely through the wilderness" (Psalm 78:52) was leading me. A chorus we had sung in former years came to mind with renewed significance:

> My Lord knows the way through the wilderness,
>
> All I need to do is to follow.
>
> Strength for the day is mine all the way,
>
> All that I need for tomorrow:
>
> My Lord knows the way through the wilderness,
>
> All I have to do is to follow.

And just as God had faithfully provided water from a rock and bread from heaven for the wandering Israelites, so he would dispense to me the necessary sustenance for my journey—and often in just as unexpected sources and ways.

How can I ever forget that special oasis at the beautiful Springs of Living Water Retreat at Richardson Springs, California! Almost out of desperation, I had set aside that week to seek God's will for whatever new role he might have for my life. Although a Bible conference was in session there, I felt the need to quietly withdraw just to hear God's voice. In the midst of an intense heat wave of 100 degrees for many days, I sought out a cool stream and sat there on a rock with God's Word in my lap and my feet in the cool flowing waters. I read, prayed and listened. Even when I tried to arrange for a counseling session with one of the conference speakers, God arranged for a long distance phone call to snatch this person from me. God wanted to speak to me in his own way, and he used John 15 as his message. How gently and beautifully the Lord reminded

God Recycles **Broken** *Dreams*

me he was the vine and I was the branch; that my only responsibility was to keep abiding in him and let his Word dwell in me. He would take care of the rest; fruit-bearing would be a natural result of this union and flow. "But Lord," I pressed, "why does it seem my life is so barren now? I feel more like a dry stick in the ground than a fruit-producing vine!"

"Oh, daughter," He explained, "you're in the pruning stage. After so much service for me, your branch has grown out quite far from me; now I'm clipping you back so you can be close to me, the vine, and allow my sap to flow through with fresh, life-giving vitality. I know it hurts; it is a painful process, but I'm pruning you back '... for greater strength and usefulness' (John 15:3). After this is all over, you will produce a bountiful harvest." This was such a refreshing revelation—like a cool drink of water to my thirsty soul—that I lingered in John 15 for weeks to follow.

In fact, after I returned from that Bible retreat, I took a ride through Napa County vineyards just to get close to the vines there; sure enough, the clusters of grapes were not to be seen on any of the long extended branches, but rather on the shorter ones which were close to the vine.

In God's perfect timing, my cherished friend in Christ, Mary Carnes, confirmed this message by sharing Andrew Murray's inspirational book, *The True Vine*. In it he explained how the eight to ten foot growth of branches are proof of its vigorous life, but it needs to be pruned because it would consume too much sap to fill the long shoots of last year's growth, and the sap must be saved for the fruit. He argues that our religious activity, our natural gifts, influence, and zeal are in danger of being unduly developed and trusted. So after each session of work, God has to bring us to the end of ourselves so that we might be aware of our helplessness and dependence upon Jesus Christ.

After ten years of wilderness, I *finally* understood the dealings of God in my life—His pruning activity. Wow! Gladly would I be cut back so that he might bring forth fruit unto his name and for his glory. To celebrate this breakthrough, Mary and Bob presented me with a beautiful grapevine, which I planted in our backyard. This became a growing lesson and reminder. And to this day whenever I see a grape, whether actual or a replication, there is an instant joy that wells up within my spirit because of all its significance.

During this reconstruction period, God spoke to me clearly by way of the grapevine. Also when I would murmur and complain against circumstances, he would patiently remind me of the fact that I was just like a simple clay pot, while he was the potter shaping me according to his choosing. The warning was, "Woe to the man who fights with his Creator. Does the pot argue with its maker? Does the clay dispute with him who forms it, saying, 'Stop, you're doing it wrong! Or the pot exclaim, 'How clumsy can you be?'" (Isaiah 45:9).

"Well, Lord, this all started with my writing a letter to you. I must say you were a long time in answering it, but at least I understood what you meant by the time you finished your reply… Oh, you're not finished yet? You say you want me to take a look at an egg? What can a simple egg teach me? Oh, well, I'm listening, Lord!"

God Recycles **Broken** *Dreams*

Chapter 3
Egg Salad Fill-in

Equally as traumatic as the breakup of my home and marriage was that long barren stretch of reconstruction. Having been an active leader in church circles for twenty years—actually often in the very center of activity—I found it most frustrating and humiliating to now find myself on the edge, or even outside, of that circle. I had led many Bible study groups, taught Sunday school classes, even trained the teachers. But now I had to sit back with the listeners and learners with just occasional requests to serve as a substitute. I had conducted Vacation Bible Schools, children's Bible Clubs and initiated Junior Church services, but now I was asked to merely assist with the music or only to monitor children in Junior Church while a much less capable and younger leader was in charge. *If they only knew how much I could help them*, I often thought. I had played either the piano or organ for church services ever since I was twelve years of age; I had even been the pianist of our Bible college chapel services for two years, but now I was just a "fill-in" when a pianist or organist had other engagements.

I will never forget the Sunday morning that I was asked to play just the prelude on the organ while the regular organist accompanied the choir with their pre-service warm-ups in their practice room. As the sanctuary was being filled with worshippers and it was time for the service to begin, I glanced up and there stood the organist next to me waiting for me to get up! As I glanced at her very pregnant condition, I wondered why I could not continue playing to spare her the cumbersome task and to spare me the humiliation.

Such was my lot for ten long years—just a "fill-in!" During that very stressful period, I must confess I often murmured and complained. Like the children of Israel longing for their former securities and desiring the leeks and onions of Egypt, I longed for my former roles and delights. "Why doesn't anyone need my service now, Lord?" I complained. "You gave me these abilities and gifts so why don't you make room for them?" And then that insidious strain of jealousy would even pose as a consultant to God, "Lord, can't you see how these younger, inexperienced workers really aren't doing a very effective job?"

It was in the throes of these frustrations of feeling overlooked by others who were "going on with the show" that God broke through with his flood-light of illumination stilling my troubled mind with these words of truth, "My daughter, these people around you are not neglecting or mistreating you. Everything is in my control, nothing is happening to you but what I am allowing." In that instant of relief, I was made to realize that it was God, my loving and wise heavenly Father, who was manipulating circumstances and people, not to hurt me but rather to purify and accomplish his purposes within me.

In humble contrition I responded, "Oh, God, if all this distress is you at work within me, forgive me for my murmuring and complaining. I'm willing to take anything from *your* hand. I yield myself as *your* handmaiden; submissive to *your* will for *your* will is my delight. Even if I never *do* anything for you again, just knowing that I am pleasing you is all that really matters. I'll be content to wait for *your* assignments in *your* time and place. As I clearly discern *your* will, I will obey. Thank *you*, Lord Jesus, for the privilege of being *yours*." The scripture, "Don't murmur against God and his dealings with you, as some of them did, for that is why God sent his angel to destroy them" (I Corinthians 10:10) was impressed indelibly upon my spirit.

Having come out on the other side of this difficult life experience, I was privileged to share the benefits of it with a singles group. Since the occasion was their Spring Thing Banquet, I was inspired to use a decorated Easter egg as the basis for my talk. We were amazed and inspired together as this "egg-head" taught us the deep truths of God.

God Recycles **Broken** *Dreams*

First, we pondered the potential of an egg. Ideally, under the proper circumstances of fertilization, this egg could become a baby chick. But just as most eggs do not become chicks—their highest fulfillment—so we humans do not usually attain our highest dreams and ideals. Yet, all is not lost, for an egg that does not become a chick is still very useful!

Before this egg is useful, however, it must first go through various treatments. Initially, the egg must be candled and graded. In the candling process, a tube light shines through it to detect any imperfections or cracks. It must have a healthy life cell. Just so, the searching light of the Holy Spirit must penetrate our inner life to be sure there is a new life in Christ and then to expose our imperfections—"Search me, O God, and know my heart; test my thoughts. Point out anything you find in me that makes you sad and lead me along the path of everlasting life" (Psalm 139:23-24).

Then this candled egg must be graded for size; some are small, others are medium, large, and even jumbo. These are actually equally valuable in that there are occasions when a small egg is more desirable than a larger one and vice versa. Just so, each of us has varying capacities and gifts, but we are equally important and needed in God's plan. "Just as there are many parts to our bodies, so it is with Christ's body. We are all parts of it, and it takes every one of us to make it complete, for we each have different work to do. So we belong to one another and each needs all the others" (Romans 12:4-5).

After the candling and grading process, the egg is boxed and then distributed to warehouses and stores. They have no say but must go where they are sent. We, too, have assignments in life. "The people of the Lord will live where they are sent" (Micah 2:5). "The steps of a good man are ordered by the Lord" (Psalm 37:23 KJV). Perhaps at times we feel all "boxed in" because of our circumstance in life. We may even be tempted to break out of the box—that confinement—but if we are to be useful, we must be patient and trusting. "Don't be impatient for the Lord to act! Keep traveling steadily along his pathway, and in due season he will honor you with every blessing..." (Psalm 37:34). Young mothers and housewives often experience this trapped, boxed-in feeling, but if they can recognize and accept this as just one stage of life, which is needful and useful in the overall plan, then it won't seem so useless and confining.

After all this preliminary treatment, finally the egg is recognized for its importance; it is now taken off the shelf and purchased by the housewife. If only the egg would know what lies ahead, it would undoubtedly prefer just staying right there on the shelf in the grocer's cooler. Without any warning, this egg is mercilessly plunged into a pan of cold water. And if that is not ruthless enough, it soon feels the flame beneath the pan. Gradually the water becomes hotter and hotter until it reaches the boiling point. The egg must wonder how it can possibly endure anymore of this treatment—the fact is, some cannot—they crack in the intense heat!

There are overwhelming experiences of sorrow and disappointment that make us feel that we, too, are drowning in the waters of our tears and suffering. And then, to add insult to injury, the heat of testing seems to be turned on, and the waters begin to boil. But if in those confusing, tempestuous times, we can just cease our struggling to listen to these words, we will be comforted: "Don't be afraid, for I have ransomed you; I have called you by name; you are mine. When you go through deep waters and great trouble, I will be with you. When you go through rivers of difficulty, you will not drown! When you walk through the fire of oppression, you will not be burned up—the flames will not consume you. For I am the Lord your God, your Savior, the Holy One of Israel" (Isaiah 43:1-3).

By now, the egg must be asking apprehensively, "What next?"

Suddenly it becomes aware of the shell breaking. And not only a breaking, but then follows a peeling—how painful and humiliating! But that is part of the process for our becoming useful—our outer shell must be broken. That self-protective façade must be cracked so that the Christ-like life can be released within. God uses whatever is needful to accomplish this very important phase of our usefulness. But again, let me remind you that you are not left alone during this difficult hour; "The Lord is close to those whose hearts are breaking..." (Psalm 34:18). The peeling is even more distasteful than the breaking because

God Recycles **Broken** *Dreams*

of the humiliating exposure of our naked selves. How we resent others gazing upon our losses and failures—that broken marriage, our wayward child, a failed business! Perhaps our pain can be lessened as we gaze upon the bruised, stripped body of our Savior hanging in full view of the boisterous crowd, for it is "… by his stripes that we are healed" (I Peter 2:24 KJV).

Surely, matters can't get much worse for me than this, the egg must be hopefully thinking. But it suddenly feels the sharp cuttings of a knife across its already peeled body. *Perhaps the housewife is cutting me into attractive wedges so that I might be used to garnish a salad… ah… Useful at last! But no… she is chopping me into small pieces*," the egg moans. And the egg is then mashed into nothingness.

Until we are aware of our nothingness without God, we are not useful *to* God. So he supervises our candling, grading, distribution and then allows the fiery trials, the breaking, peeling, cutting, and mashing that we might truly become useful. Like John, we should pray, "He must increase, but I must decrease (John 3:30 KJV). These cuttings could represent the cutting criticisms of bystanders who really do not understand one's sufferings. Also it could include the pruning knife of the divine husbandman. The mashings are the dealings of the Holy Spirit in our lives, when all the "I can's" and the "I am's" are mashed, leaving just the Christ-like life within us.

Now that the egg has been mashed into nothingness, the housewife mixes mayonnaise with it, and it becomes delicious egg salad with which she prepares egg salad sandwiches for her hungry family. So as the oil of joy (Isaiah 61:1-3) of the Holy Spirit blends our mashed nothingness with the life of Christ within, we become food and nourishment for hungry souls.

That I was a "fill-in" was God's humorous punchline. For during my wilderness journey, my main complaint to God had been, "Why do I have to be just a 'fill-in'—a 'fill-in' for Sunday School teachers, a 'fill-in' for Junior Church workers, a 'fill-in' pianist or organist—when in previous years I had been completely in charge of such roles. So with a big understanding smile on his loving face, God replied, "What good is a sandwich without the 'fill-in'!"

God always does have the final word, even if it is with an "egg-head"! "Thanks, Father, for making it so simple!"

Chapter 4
Single Bliss

The latest addition to my bedroom "art gallery" is a magnificent waterfall scene surrounded by stately pine trees, and what draws my attention even more than the gorgeous picture are these words: "The world is such that what may appear to be an end is only a new beginning."

One winter a merciless frost killed one of the beautiful lavender fuchsia bushes growing in our backyard. Reluctant to cut down my familiar flower friend, I just left it to itself. Much to my joy, a few months later I noticed that a healthy new green shoot had sprouted from what appeared to be a dead stalk.

Both Jesus Christ and St. Paul taught this principle of new life coming forth out of death by alluding to the seed of corn, which after being planted must die to its old form before a new plant springs forth (John 12:24, I Corinthians 15:36). And how dramatically God the Father illustrated this eternal truth with the resurrection of Jesus Christ!

I felt like I, too, had been buried—in a tomb of gloom, but I also experienced a resurrection of new hope and life in Christ Jesus. "Therefore if any man be in Christ he is a new creature; old things are passed away; behold, all things are become new" (II Corinthians 5:17 KJV). I learned that the same God who causes the wrath of man to praise him (Psalm 76:10) can also convert sorrow into joy (Isaiah 61:3) and even marital tragedy into single bliss.

As I entered this new land of "single bliss," I moved along with cautious uncertainty. Upon the archway of the hypothetical gate, I observed this challenging statement, "Godliness with contentment is great gain" (I Timothy 6:6

KJV). "Although I've lost a lot," I mused, "somehow I feel I still have what really matters most, and I even sense a surge of expectancy of better days ahead!"

Strolling along the garden path, I came to a quiet reflecting pool. It was a calming, refreshing experience. I was amazed to learn the clear waters were transformed tears: "When they walk through the Valley of Weeping it will become a place of springs where pools of blessing and refreshment collect after rains" (Psalm 84:6).

Occasionally I would encounter fellow travelers in this land who would welcome me into their times of sharing. Some were in a pit of bitter despair while others were treading more carefully. One of them was saying, "You know it really isn't so much what happens to us in life that counts but rather how we react to those happenings."

"Yes," I added, "We can become bitter or better, and that depends on our attitudes toward life. It helps me to praise God for what's left rather than complain about what's gone." By sharing our common experiences of both the hazards encountered and the lessons learned, we were mutually strengthened.

Scanning the scenery, I was intrigued by the colorful butterflies flitting about so effortlessly. "But," I reminisced, "life was not always so light and lively for these lovely creatures; they, too, have had their caterpillar stage and then those dark days of obscurity within the chrysalis. They, too, experienced that life-and-death struggle of having to break through the pupa shell. And that very process of struggle is the action that pumps fluids into the veins of their wings making possible this flight of ecstasy. *Ah, beautiful flying gems, you were born to fly, and so was I.*

Nearing the noon hour in the Land of Single Bliss, I sought out an attractive restaurant. It would have added to the pleasure of the occasion to have dined with someone, but in the absence of such a luxury I chose not to give up eating! Oh—the hostess is addressing me searchingly, "Are you alone?"

Thinking of the plight of all my fellow travelers and refusing to succumb to self-pity, I replied firmly and informatively, "No, there are forty-three million of us." (There really are that many singles in the United States.)

God Recycles **Broken** *Dreams*

After having placed my order, I must admit I found it rather boring just to sip from the glass of water. "I hope I can find someone to accompany me the next time I eat out, or maybe someone would even think to invite me. Oh well, a little bit of wishful thinking goes a long way to brighten the day!"

I must be honest and admit that there have been long, lonely stretches in this Land of Single Bliss—like that two-hundred-mile car trek along the Pacific coast on that bleak Saturday. Seeing family groups and couples enjoying the ocean spray certainly did cause a watery mist to swell into my eyes: and that unforgettable experience of going to the Santa Cruz boardwalk—just wanting to mingle with a carefree crowd. But how much companionship can a corn dog or candied apple offer?

Sitting on a park bench in this new land, I somehow sensed the presence of my friend Jesus Christ, so we naturally started sharing. "Jesus," I began, "when I felt the responsibilities of married life, I secretly wished you had been married during your earthly life so that you could have understood all the implications of such a relationship. But now, I'm rather glad you were single because I feel somehow you really understand my lonely moments."

To which he replied, "Yes, I often was alone, even deserted by my closest friends; yet I really was never alone, for my Father was always with me (John 16:32). And so he will always be with you."

Walking along, I turned on my portable radio. A Christian psychologist was speaking, and just at that moment he was commenting on a listener's letter. This listener was evidently a lonely single. The Christian psychologist commented, "Let me encourage you to realize that for every letter I receive from a distressed single, I receive at least three from married listeners pleading for help to get out of the mess they are in. So I would say enjoy your freedom because there are many things worse than being single, and one them is being married to the wrong person."

Well, that was something to write down in the positive ledger of my notebook. In fact, that ledger was becoming overcrowded with momentos being accumulated along the way. Under the heading of *Advantages of Living in the Land of Single Bliss*, were to be found such entries as:

- ✓ Freedom in Planning Schedule
- ✓ Lots More Closet and Drawer Space
- ✓ Independence in Coming and Going
- ✓ Less Structured Meal Times
- ✓ Liberties in Planning Budget

I noticed a little footnote that cautioned me, "With new freedom, there are new responsibilities," and if I would let myself glance over to the other side of the ledger, sure enough, I was reminded of some of these:

- ✓ Must Be My Own 'Fixer-Upper"
- ✓ Vexations of Tax Forms
- ✓ Yard Work and House Repair
- ✓ Car Care
- ✓ Handle All Financial Matters

In the midst of considering all the assets and liabilities of my new position, there were times of wishful thinking for companionship—especially during those lonely weekends when the routine of the work week suddenly came to a halt. My whole being would cry out for a change of pace, place and persons… but with whom?

"Ouch! What was that? Oh, one of cupid's darts. Where did it come from?"

One of cupid's helpers had clipped an ad in the Pen Pal section of a newspaper which read, "Oklahoma male, 5'9", 180 lb., blue eyes, brown hair, Christian, good-looking, easy to get along with, non-smoker and non-drinker, marriage-minded with Christian lady in her 40's."

Although this sounded appealing, and I received complimentary letters in response to my letter and photo, I felt restraints within my spirit to not pursue any further interest. So—cupid's dart fell with a thud.

God Recycles **Broken** *Dreams*

Later another gentleman from southern California who had learned of me through unique circumstances made numerous attempts toward friendship. At first he seemed like a dream come true; but the more he revealed his values, the more I perceived that we were more than just geographical miles apart. In spite of all the nice-to-hear compliments, I knew it would be risky to continue the correspondence.

So I gave all my frustrations and disappointments to the Lord. "Thank you, Father, for protecting me from possible sorrow. If you want me to have a companion, he will have to come through your arrangement, not mine!"

As I waited quietly in his presence, I heard him reply, "My daughter, I have been jealous over my relationship with you, and I know you have guarded and cherished your relationship with me. I love you, my daughter, and desire you to stay close to me. I will protect and bless you with blessings and joys far beyond anything earthly relationships can provide."

In a new dimension, I experienced the truth of, "For your Creator will be your husband. The Lord of hosts is his name; He is your Redeemer, the Holy One of Israel, the God of all the earth" (Isaiah 54:5). At that moment, I reaffirmed that any new friendship would have to be born of God and result in a strengthening of our mutual love for God (I Corinthians 7:32-35).

So with a bit more wisdom concerning the ways and wiles of this new land, I resumed my journey. To compensate for the added pressures of responsibilities, I would plan for little trips or treats, such as a musical concert, an Oakland A's game or an Ice Capades Show. I recall desiring to attend the Royal Lipizzan Stallion Show at the Oakland Coliseum, but admission prices were somewhat prohibitive for me. I "just happened" to tune in to a local radio station which was sponsoring a "Horse Sense" contest for which listeners were urged to write an essay on "How to Run our Country," and the winner would receive free tickets to the magnificent Lipizzan show. I responded by proposing ways to rebuild our country upon the bedrock of God's Word—upon integrity, humility, and moral justice. It was gratifying to be the winner of four tickets!

Besides these periodic "pick-ups" for my morale, I had discovered a new delight in remembering myself on my birthday and wedding anniversary dates with a "Happy birthday to Me!" and "Happy anniversary to Me! I have always enjoyed being thoughtful of others on their special days, but somehow I had neglected myself! How can we love others if we don't love ourselves! Jesus taught, "Love thy neighbor as thyself" (Matthew 19:19 KJV). So to celebrate each birthday and wedding anniversary, I indulge in a gift to myself. When I ask myself, "Can I afford to buy it?" the answer comes back emphatically, "You can't afford not to!"

I recall my first such purchase. It was in that period of my stressful separation. As I gazed upon that glittering aurora borealis necklace, with its handsome price tag (actually less than $20), my logical reasoning was holding the reins, but my spirit burst forth with, "You deserve every shimmering twinkle of new hope reflected in that lovely necklace!" Within moments, I was its happy owner.

And that was just the first of many other tokens of love from me to me, such as a graceful swan centerpiece, a waffle and pancake griddle and a set of pretty dishes. But not only material things—I recall a fantastic anniversary celebration at beautiful Lake Tahoe where the showman Liberace performed in person, along with the Korean Angels and a spectacular display of dancing waters. As I would enjoy some of these exhilarating experiences, I often would chuckle to myself, "I believe I'm having more fun than some of my married friends!"

The unforgettable splurge was on my 25th wedding anniversary, which splashed me all the way to Hawaii. I realize it sounds almost hilarious—celebrating a 25th wedding anniversary in Hawaii—alone, but what a joyful, delightful experience! I had often envisioned the traditional "Open House" silver anniversary celebration. But now, rather than bemoan my disappointment, why not plan something even more grandiose? How, on a very limited salary, did I ever manage to go to Hawaii? That is an exciting story!

In the spring of 1975, I received a brochure in the mail describing a Great World Christian convention to be held in Anaheim, California, in July and

God Recycles **Broken** *Dreams*

from there an extended convention in Hawaii. A desire to go almost exploded within my heart. "Oh, Father, how I would love to attend those affairs! But, it says here, Lord, that a $50 deposit has to be sent in by April 15, and you know how April has been a lean month for me because of taxes due."

The Lord seemed to say, "Don't you know as you delight yourself in me that I not only give you the desires of your heart, but I also *fill* them (Psalm 37:4)? Now why do you limit me just because it's tax month? Don't you know I have unlimited resources? (Have you forgotten how my Son got his tax money from a fish?) Just keep in mind that I specialize in things that seem impossible" (Mark 10:27).

"Oh, Lord, I'm so excited! I know you are going to make a way for me. I can already see myself there in beautiful Honolulu—get that lei ready!"

As I started thinking, praying, talking Hawaii, not only did the $50 deposit come together miraculously, but also the balance that was due by the end of June—the bulk of it coming from my income tax refund, which I'm sure the Lord expedited.

I will never forget the morning of my departure when Kevin, my mischievous nephew, with his friend, Mark, pulled into my driveway with the siren blowing on what had been a police car. Wearing an attractive white pants suit that had been purchased during the previous summer sale for "some special occasion," I dashed outside, "Please, Kevin, cool it; I'm excited enough without all that noise!"

He just grinned back at me.

Having checked my luggage at the Oakland Airport, I ordered a glass of grapefruit juice at the cafeteria. Somewhat stunned by the cost of sixty-nine cents for just a glassful, I nevertheless paid the cashier and sat down at a nearby table. "Oh thank you, Father, for this wonderful joy of being able to go to Anaheim and then to Hawaii!"

As I glanced down at the floor, I could hardly believe my eyes, for there were two quarters and two dimes! Yes, seventy cents! "Oh, Father, I know this is just a token of how you plan to take care of me during this whole joyous adventure! Thank you."

At the Burbank Airport, I was met by my sister, Violet, and then whisked away to her apartment. But not for long, for Violet, being a globe-trotter, just cannot justify "wasting" one's time eating, sleeping, or just sitting around making conversation when the whole big wonderful world is waiting to be explored. So with her skillful scheduling, I enjoyed quite a prelude to the Anaheim convention by going to the quaint Danish community of Solvang (I learned from experience that Danish pastries last for a minute on the lips and forever on the hips); also, we went to the beautiful Huntington Library with its palatial gardens and famous paintings, and to the well-known Forest Lawn Cemetery in Glendale with all its magnificent art.

After an inspiring week of services at Anaheim with 10,000 participants filling that huge convention center, I was more eager than ever for that lift-off to Hawaii.

Having checked my baggage at the Los Angeles airport, boarding that jumbo jet and fastening my seat belt, I glanced at the couple sitting beside me and endeavored to get acquainted. I learned we had some mutual interests—they were school teachers, had attended the Anaheim convention, and were registered for the extension in Hawaii. But what almost startled me was the wife's sharing, "We decided to go to Hawaii for our 25th wedding anniversary."

I just could not bring myself to divulge my secret that this, too, was my 25th wedding anniversary celebration—only mine was alone. But before we even landed in Honolulu, observing their lack of communication, I could almost predict who was going to enjoy this adventure the most!

What a thrilling sight it was to focus in on the mounds of Hawaiian Islands among the azure blue Pacific as our jet descended. Greeted with a gorgeous lei, fragrant with yellow pulmerias and pink carnations, I felt like a *somebody* already! Our group was then escorted to the impressive Ala Moana Hotel.

All that week my spirit absorbed so many delectable sights and sounds that I remained feasting on the memories for a long time. There were the inspi-

God Recycles **Broken** *Dreams*

rational Bible seminars conducted in the hotel ballroom during which the islanders, so humbly beautiful, joined with us "mainlanders" in worshipping the Lord. One of the islanders learned of my fondness of mangoes and brought several large luscious ones to the hotel the following day.

In between services, I enjoyed relaxing at the famous Waikiki Beach with its white sands and warm ocean waters that looked like molten aquamarine jewels. Wherever one went, there were the fragrant flowers and flowing music—what a romantic paradise! "How nice it would be to have a husband by my side," I reflected, "but," added hastily, "at least *I'm* here, and that's half the fun."

Taking a tour of Pearl Harbor and seeing the remains of the historic battleship, the U.S.S. Arizona, with its monument over the watery grave of 1,181 servicemen was quite a sobering experience. Seeing the vast pineapple plantation, all hand-planted and hand-harvested, was quite a learning event; realizing a pineapple takes from eighteen to twenty-two months to ripen made me appreciate their price more.

Our convention climaxed with a grand banquet in an almost fairyland setting of an exotic hotel ballroom. Chandeliers have always intrigued me, but the exquisite chandeliers in Hawaiian hotels are breathtakingly beautiful. The colorful muumuus worn by the ladies, and the floral designed shirts worn by the men created an unforgettable scene.

In the midst of this festive atmosphere, I caught a glimpse of the couple "celebrating" their 25th wedding anniversary. I purposely avoided asking them if they had enjoyed their week in Hawaii, for the answer was all too obvious. *How sad to come all the way to Hawaii—this romantic paradise—with 'dead batteries,'* I thought, *and not even to have allowed this beautiful atmosphere to generate a spark!* I was sad for them.

This brought to mind an injury I had suffered several years prior to this time. I had fallen on some steps, and as a result sprained one ankle and broke the other. I often recall the physician's words: "Ruth, you'll find this sprained one will give you a lot more trouble than the broken one, for a clean break allows for a thorough healing whereas the sprain will give you periodic stress." How applicable to human relationships!

"Father, I know the sorrow and pain of a strained relationship. Although I did not choose a break, I thank you for your healing graces that make possible this "Single Bliss"—especially under your protective love and care. Please let every hurting heart know that you are very close to them through your Son Jesus Christ."

God Recycles **Broken** *Dreams*

Chapter 5
Half-price Baby

There seems to be an insatiable quest for human beings to trace back to their roots—and often with that hidden desire to establish proof of royal or aristocratic ancestry. I cannot boast of royal or aristocratic ancestry. I cannot boast a royal bloodline, for my forefathers were very ordinary people. (Perhaps the closest my relatives came to royalty was serving them: my maternal grandfather served as bodyguard to Kaiser Wilhelm of Germany, and one of my great-uncles traveled aboard ship with Theodore Roosevelt.) However, it is with humble pride that I claim roots that sought out rich, productive soil—roots that were deeply entwined in values of integrity and perseverance—roots that provided life-giving sustenance for sturdy character and fruitful accomplishments. And in order to maintain this perennial life force, these roots tapped the very source of life— God himself—through a deep respect for God's Word and an allegiance to Jesus Christ as Lord of life.

Rather than getting their roots entangled with the worldly, humanistic and materialistic philosophies of their day and age, my grandparents were actively engaged in promoting and supporting the Kingdom of God. My mother shared with me how her parents would often provide lodging for itinerant ministers and also started and maintained a spiritual lighthouse in an unchurched German village. One of my godly great-grandmothers would often sit in her rocking chair with handwork on her lap and a hymn of praise on her lips—singing scriptures to the Lord. Also, one of my great-aunts served as a missionary from Germany to Africa in the early 1900s.

Some of my Huguenot forefathers were driven out of France under religious persecutions of Ludwig XIV, and found refuge in East Prussia. My grandparents suffered through the Russian invasion of Germany in World War I while my mother, but a young girl at the time, was evacuated to a place of safety for her schooling. Again during World War II my aging grandparents, together with my Aunt Hildegard and Uncle Franz, had to flee from their homes that had been bombed by the Russians. At one point because of my Uncle's refusal to align with the Nazi philosophy, he was sent to a hard labor camp.

After months of near starvation and death, and very concerned about the welfare of his family, he made a desperate escape. With swollen feet and starving body, he persevered through deep snow over many dangerous miles. Having to cross a lake that was guarded by Russians, he prayed for God's special protection. His valiant faith was rewarded with God dispatching such a heavy blanket of fog over the lake region that the Russians were unaware of my uncle's safe crossing. Finally with great gratitude to God, he was tearfully reunited with his family. But after just a brief period of security, their home was bombed again so they sought refuge in a cellar and later in a large public bomb shelter.

Even after the war ceased, my relatives still suffered the devastating ravages of home, possessions, and health; but with steadfast faith and courage, they became established again. In their retired years, Aunt Hildegard and Uncle Franz spent much of their time traveling throughout Germany ministering God's Word through teaching seminars and also with organ and violin presentations.

It was in God's providence that my father's relatives were adventurous enough to migrate to the United States of America, giving their posterity roots

God Recycles Broken Dreams

in "the land of promise and opportunity." So it was in 1923 that my parents, as newlyweds braving a stormy Atlantic voyage, caught sight of the Statue of Liberty in New York Harbor. Having sold all their belongings in exchange for their passage on the ship, they survived many hardships in this new land with their indomitable faith in God intact. There were also humorous moments in this new situation, such as when my mother saw her first hot dog stand. Frightened, she clutched my father's arm with, "Ach, Hansel, da sind heise Hunde!"

She was shocked to think people in this new country would eat heated dogs! But in due time, Mother became Americanized enough to serve hot dogs for our lunches.

After many trying circumstances, although brightened by the birth of their firstborn son, John Samuel, my parents were invited by German Baptist friends to settle in the cozy village of Stuyvesant Falls, New York, along the Hudson River. Here my parents were warmly received and loved. My father was recognized as a lay minister and frequently shared God's Word with the German fellowship there. While in that community, my parents had an early Christmas present one year with the birth of my sister Violet. But as joys and sorrows so often travel together, a drunken driver soon crashed into my father's 1925 Model T Ford, breaking his arm, severing a finger, and causing extensive damage to his car. Still my parents often referred to that Christmas as one of their most unforgettable because of the many tokens of Christian love showered upon them during that time of crisis.

Just thirteen months after that memorable Christmas is when it all really began—as far as I was concerned. It was a cold Sunday morning in January—so cold that the waters of the picturesque Stuyvesant Falls became a frozen cascade. Inside a cozy little yellow cottage situated on the bank of this temporarily quieted falls, there was quite a stir of activity. An experienced German midwife was keeping watch with my mother while my father hastily hurried off to summon the village doctor. But in typical fashion, I was in a hurry and couldn't wait for the doctor to arrive, so I made my debut into this big world without his assistance. Upon his arrival, he merely examined me with satisfaction and then said to my father, "Since I was not here in time for the delivery, I shall only charge you half of my regular twenty-five-dollar fee; you owe me just twelve dollars and fifty cents."

So I came into the world at a half-price fare! I have often wondered if this was not prophetic; but I will tell you more about that later.

So even though I was not born in a German castle or an American mansion, I was born of loving, God-fearing parents. It was just in recent months that I learned of my parents' sacred request accompanying the birth of each of their five children; for each child they would ask God for an appropriate scripture. And to my delight, I learned that the scripture attending my birth was one already well-loved and underlined in my own Bible: "The Lord is the portion of mine inheritance and of my cup: thou maintainest my lot. The lines are fallen unto me in pleasant places; yea, I have a goodly heritage" (Psalm 16:5-6 KJV).

Although my parents were unable to leave us a monetary legacy, they gave us a priceless heritage that I would not exchange for a million-dollar inheritance (although I would gladly accept the latter as a fringe benefit).

I have a lovely hanging on my bedroom wall depicting a tree with exposed roots and birds soaring in the blue sky; it bears these words: "There are only two lasting things we can leave our children… one is roots… the other is wings."

Desiring more economic stability and educational opportunity for his children, my father moved his family from the little village of Stuyvesant Falls northward to the industrial city of Schenectady, New York, home of the General Electric Company. Arriving there at the tail end of the depression years, my father struggled to keep bread and butter on the table for his family (in spite of the fact that butter cost only one dollar for three pounds

God Recycles Broken Dreams

at that time). It is with mingled feelings of pain and gratitude that I recall his having to leave his car parked in the driveway because of lack of money for license and gas, and pedal his old bike in below-freezing temperatures to his WPA job of repairing roads. Commuting and working in such temperatures resulted in frostbitten ears. I can remember as a very young child standing in line for our rations of dried beans and powdered milk and distasteful canned meat. But my parents, having their roots in the resources of the eternal God, always provided our basic needs. "…In all my years I have never seen the Lord forsake a man who loves Him; nor have I seen the children of the godly go hungry" (Psalm 37:25). "Reverence for God gives a man deep strength; his children have a place of refuge and security" (Proverbs 14:26). I am sure because of the security my father provided for us, I have found it easy to transfer that trust to my heavenly Father.

One is tempted to almost glamorize one's parents who were so sacrificial, especially now that they are in Heaven, but I am increasingly aware that my parents grappled with common problems and with limited human under-standing—at times even with misunderstandings. But love and forgiveness prevailed, and that is the best household cement. "And above all these, put on love, which binds everything together in perfect harmony" (Colossians 3:14). "…Love makes up for many of your faults" (I Peter 4:8).

Although my father was a strict disciplinarian, he tempered this with many hours of family fun. Often on a Saturday afternoon in the summer when housework and weeding the garden had been completed, we would pile into our '36 Plymouth and head for one of the several beautiful lakes within easy driving distance for a swim, boating and a scrumptious picnic lunch packed by mother. Also, we would be assured an annual visit to our country cousins in Owego, New York, and then another visit to our relatives in the big metrop-olis of New York City. While in the big city, Dad would take us to the Bronx Zoo and the World's Fair when in operation there. Also, we would make periodic treks to the ocean shore in New Jersey to visit my mother's only relatives living in America. I recall getting up at three in the morning—without being coaxed—and setting off on our fourteen-hour trip.

Among my most cherished childhood memories are those of our Christmas Eve celebrations. As darkness deepened in the evening, the lights of our Christmas tree and the glow in our hearts would shine all the more brightly. Our celebration would begin with Dad's reading of the Christmas story out of the German family Bible, then we would kneel as a family and one by one offer a prayer of gratitude to our Lord for sending the Christ-child to earth. I thought Dad always made the longest prayers on that occasion! Gathering around our old-fashioned pump organ and singing Christmas carols was next; the final number always had to be "Stille Nacht, Heilige Nacht"—sung in German. Finally, after what seemed like forever, we were ready for our exchange of gifts, which always reflected sacrificial love. Such practical items as warm PJs, mittens, and slippers were joyfully received. Also, we always looked forward to the new games, such as Chinese checkers, Jack Straws, and Monopoly (now we would no longer have to pay twenty-five cents to borrow our neighbor's set).

The Christmas when I was given a used ten-button bass accordion, and when my sister and I were presented with a used Underwood typewriter (which was still in use twenty-five years later) I was almost ecstatic. We children had scraped together our pennies and dimes to purchase some dessert dishes for Mother and perhaps a new tie for Daddy. After the opening of our gifts, Mother would lead us to the dining room buffet which boasted a colorful array of "Bunten Teller" (literally, "fancy dishes"), in which were nuts, candies, home-made Christmas cookies, and an orange. Each one of us had his own "fancy dish" with his name tag on it; we guarded these carefully.

There were some very meager Christmas celebrations, too. I shall never forget one year, when after our usual Bible and prayer time, there were no gifts

God Recycles **Broken** *Dreams*

to be opened, and with sad, heavy hearts we children dragged ourselves to bed. (I am sure our parents' hearts were even heavier). We had hardly gotten tucked in between our feather beds when a knock was heard on our front door, with an exchange of happy voices. Not able to constrain our curiosity, we tiptoed downstairs, and there to our joyful surprise was an assortment of fine used toys that had been collected by a kind, understanding family. What a happy ending for us all!

Another early childhood memory was my nightly bedtime wish. Mother and Dad seemed always to get a delight out of questioning me each evening in German, "Und was villst du haben wenn du aufwachst?" (And what do you want to have when you grow up)?

Consistently, my reply would be, "Eine ganze Stube woll kleine Madchen und eine ganze Stube voll kleine Jungens." (A whole room full of little girls and a whole room full of little boys).

And I literally envisioned them filling a room from floor to ceiling. Perhaps this was prophetic of my teaching children in my adult years. There were times when I taught Bible Clubs when almost every inch of floor space was covered with these little ones, but they never stacked up to the ceiling!

Besides our family work times, hard times, and fun times, we children enjoyed just good old-fashioned neighborhood fun. We played hide-and-seek, giant steps, and all kinds of ball games in the neighboring schoolyard. In winter, it was sledding down the packed snow on our hilly street (until a cranky neighbor would call for the city sanding crew to curtail our fun), and ice-skating in the flooded ice-rink on the schoolyard. All this wholesome out-of-door fun was quite in contrast to the boredom experienced by our youth today—victims of the TV and Internet.

Probably all of us have at some time been aware of a "gas war," but I can remember an even more gratifying war and that was the "ice cream wars," when we could buy a super-duper large dip for just three cents! Frequently, preceding an occasional ice cream treat, Dad would drive us to Central Park where we would watch with quiet enthrallment the magnificent fountain in the center of the man-made lake. I would sometimes feel I had been transported to fantasyland as I watched the multi-colored lights play upon the cascading waters.

Our annual sauerkraut-making day was another traditional family project. Several bushels of cabbage heads would be cleaned, cut and shredded on a special board; we then sprinkled them with salt and stomped them down into a fifty-gallon crock. One of the rewards of shoveling coal on the furnace fire in those wintry evenings was to be able to sample the sauerkraut that was processing in the basement!

But with all those memories even more outstanding are the spiritual paths on which our parents led us. My father's choices of where to live always staked out three priorities: proximity to his job, availability of good schools, and access to an evangelical church. My path was not flanked by phony TV personalities (with all due respect for the genuine ones), or by dazzling movie stars, but I was surrounded by a stalwart army of godly pastors, sacrificial missionaries, zealous evangelists and a warm fellowship of believers. These were often dinner and over-night guests in our home. Many times these servants of God would place their hand of blessing upon my head and confirm what God had already whispered in my spirit, "Ruth, God has a special work for you to do in his Kingdom; always stay close to Him."

It was almost impossible to be detoured on a <u>self</u>-fulfillment trip with such holy influences and challenges to be <u>God</u>-filled.

Not only were my parents active in our local church, but my father's love for God and people often led him to participate in services, rallies, and camp meetings of other Bible-believing groups. This expanded and enriched my spiritual heritage since I was always Dad's "tag-along." Hearing such men of God as E. Stanley Jones, Gypsy Smith, Homer Rodeaver with his golden

God Recycles **Broken** *Dreams*

trombone, and the successful businessman, R.G. LeTourneau, was part of my priceless heritage.

As part of my spiritual exercise during my teen years, I would go along with my father and other dedicated Christians on Saturday evenings to the bowery section of Albany, New York. I played my accordion for these open-air services, and what a joy it was to witness God's transforming power in these licentious lives!

Speaking of camp-meeting days arouses a flood of memories of smells, sounds and sights. I can still smell the freshly strewn straw on the aisles of the open tabernacle. I can hear the rising bell that would announce the daily service and meal schedules. I can still feel the prickly straw mats on which we slept in the girls' dorm and almost shiver again to recall that cold wash water from the pump house. But most of all, I recall with eternal gratitude the anointed ministry of God's Word by evangelists, gospel singers and instrumentalists. In my early teens, I would stay at these camp meetings for two weeks at a time waiting on tables to earn my room and board. Having fellowship with so many wonderful people from so many different places made this all seem like a foretaste of Heaven itself.

Attending Richland Camp Meeting, located near Lake Ontario in upper New York State, afforded the first train ride for my sister Violet and me. What an unforgettable adventure that was! Feeling somewhat apprehensive that we would miss the brief stop at Richland station, we were relieved to hear the conductor call out, "The next stop is Richland—everyone for Richland, get ready for the next stop."

So rather excitedly, with the train still in motion, we reached up to the overhead racks to pull down our large clumsy suitcases. But in our excitement, Violet's suitcase opened up—with all her clothing, hangers and toilet articles scattering in all directions. It all happened so unexpectedly and looked so ridiculous that I just burst into uncontrollable laughter. Somehow, though, we managed to get all the items gathered together in helter-skelter fashion and off the train in time.

Sensing God's call upon my life, but also realizing my parents' inability to support any of their children through college, I sought employment in the General Electric Company upon graduation from high school. Having been an honor student with a major in mathematics and science, I was hired as a lab assistant in the engineering laboratory. For two years I saved very scrupulously as much of my weekly check as possible, just taking out the Lord's tithe. The only indebtedness I allowed myself during this period was for a used 120-bass accordion—the fulfillment of a childhood dream.

This two-year interim between high school and Bible college was not only a time of financial necessity but also of spiritual preparation. It was as if God was setting me apart unto himself. Rather than take the convenient bus to work, I chose to walk the three miles to and from work. Not only did this add to my college fund, it also gave me time and space for communion with my Lord. Having an insatiable desire for God's Word, I would memorize sheets of topically arranged scriptures as I walked to and from work, thereby hiding away hundreds of promises that have held me steady all through life. Also, I typed out and memorized such hymns as:

> How firm a foundation, ye saints of the Lord
>
> Is laid for your faith in his excellent Word!
>
> What more can he say than to you he hath said
>
> To you, who for refuge to Jesus have fled?
>
> Fear not, I am with thee, O be not dismayed,
>
> For I am thy God, I will still give thee aid;
>
> I'll strengthen thee, help thee, and cause thee to stand,
>
> Upheld by my gracious omnipotent hand.

God Recycles **Broken** *Dreams*

When thro' the deep waters I call thee to go,

The rivers of sorrow shall not overflow;

For I will be with thee thy trials to bless.

And sanctify to thee thy deepest distress.

When thro' fiery trials thy pathway shall lie,

My grace, all-sufficient, shall be thy supply,

The flames shall not hurt thee: I only design

Thy dross to consume, and thy gold to refine.

Then after returning home from work and enjoying one of Mother's good suppers, I would retreat to my bedroom for more of God's Word and a time of prayer.

With so much flowing in of God's grace and blessing, there had to be an outflow; otherwise, I would have become like the Dead Sea which receives waters but none pour out. Someone has said, "Impression without expression spells depression." During this time I was appointed youth leader of our church, and as part of that responsibility I often shared a message from God's Word in the Sunday evening youth service. Also I would be called upon to share inspirations in neighboring churches and youth meetings.

It was following such a service, just three months prior to my entering college that the Lord challenged me to literally practice what I had preached. I had fervently exhorted the youth to fully consecrate their lives and everything they had to God's care and control. As a result, I quoted Frances Havergal's beautiful hymn of consecration:

Take my life, and let it be consecrated, Lord, to Thee;

Take my hands, and let them move at the impulse of Thy love.

Take my feet, and let them be swift and beautiful for Thee;

Take my voice, and let me sing always, only for my King.

Take my silver and my gold, not a mite would I withhold;

Take my moments and my days, let them flow in ceaseless praise,

Take my will and make it Thine, it shall be no longer mine;

Take my heart, it is Thine own, it shall be Thy royal throne.

That very next day, God tested my faith by asking me if I truly meant the words of this hymn—especially the part, "Take my silver and my gold, not a mite would I withhold." I was overwhelmed and frightened, but I will share with you in the next chapter how this was resolved.

"I want to thank you, Father, for my rich heritage in you, and I pray for parents everywhere; may they seek your abundant resources for their difficult but rewarding tasks."

God Recycles **Broken** *Dreams*

Chapter 6
The Five-hundred-dollar Investment

Finally, after nearly two years of skimping and saving, I was able to accumulate $500 in my savings account, which was the amount necessary to cover my first year at a Bible college. But suddenly my security was seemingly shattered by an overwhelming request from God to my heart, "Would you be willing to let me have that $500 for a missionary project?"

"But, Lord," I explained, "I've saved this money so that I might go to Bible college to prepare for your work. Now I'm really confused, Lord, so please help me know for sure if this is truly you or just a passing notion. I need a week to prayerfully seek your will about this!"

There was too much at stake to make a hasty decision about this, and it was too awesome an experience to share with anyone—not even my Christian parents or godly pastor; this was something that had to be worked out between God and me. I have found that God is very patient with us whenever we are in doubt about a matter; in fact, he will do his best to clarify the issue if we truly desire to know his will.

And God revealed to me that it was, indeed, his will for me to relinquish my $500 savings and to give it to our denomination's missionary fund. First, he had spoken to me within my spirit, and since God is spirit and I am created in his image, he must communicate with my spirit. Secondly, it was not by chance that my daily devotional reading that particular week was leading me through the epistle of II Corinthians, especially through chapters 8 and 9 where Paul commended the Christians at Corinth for assisting believers elsewhere in their material needs "…that your abundance may be a supply for their want…" (8:14 KJV), and reminding them that Jesus Christ "…though he was rich, yet for your sakes he became poor, that ye, through his poverty, might be rich (8:9 KJV)." Then I was reminded in chapter 8, verse 6, "He which soweth sparingly shall reap also sparingly; and he which soweth bountifully shall reap also bountifully," and in verse 7 KJV…"Give, not grudgingly, or of necessity: for God loveth a cheerful giver." The message was getting through.

Then to help clarify the need, our weekly denominational periodical arrived in the mail and contained a plea for added contributions to the missionary support fund which was at low ebb. So by the end of that memorable week, I knew without a doubt that God was asking me for my savings, and it was with great ecstatic joy that I went to the bank during my lunch hour and had the teller write out a cashier's check for $500. I am sure this was routine for her, but she was completely unaware of the transfer of funds that was taking place into the Bank of Heaven, nor did she realize the "sky-high" interest I would receive from that investment of faith (Matthew 6:19-21,33), which happens to be a very real concern. I realized years later that this whole experience was a test of my faith in the realm of finances.

Sixteen out of thirty-eight parables that Jesus taught dealt with money. For every verse Jesus taught about prayer, there are seven which have reference to money. Actually, he spoke five times more about money than any other topic. With many, our piety stops at the pocketbook, but unless God controls our wallet, he does not really control us. He is either Lord *of* all, or not Lord *at* all.

So instead of having my first year of Bible college fully paid, I arrived on campus with a meager $75 for tuition and board. But I had the backing of God's integrity—he just wanted my vote of confidence in his handling of my finances. There were times, I must admit, during those four years of college

God Recycles **Broken** *Dreams*

that I wondered how my needs would be met. But my divine Financier always had the accounts in control and was never late in coming to my rescue.

I'll never forget that first Thanksgiving vacation when my fellow classmates were eagerly making plans to spend the holidays with their families. It looked like I was going to have to remain in the girls' dorm for lack of bus fare home. No one but God knew that I did not have one cent for that two-hundred mile trip, but he very capably and speedily handled that dilemma. Returning to my dorm room after our last class before dismissal for the holiday, I found an envelope on my desk with $10 inside—just what I needed to travel home! Since that was given anonymously, I could only praise God and ask him to bless the gracious giver.

Then there was that six-week period in my sophomore year when sickness struck our home. This necessitated my leaving school along with my part-time job to help care for my precious father, who was a victim of terminal cancer. Not only shall I always treasure the memories of those last days together with my godly father, but also the recollection of how God again miraculously supplied my financial need. Having missed six weeks income and payment on my school bill was naturally a concern. Upon my return to college, the dean called me into his office and informed me that two individuals had approached him with gifts of $100 each to be applied to my account. How grateful I was!

During the summer before my senior year, I was newly settled into a good paying job in Washington, D.C. when I received a call from home again informing me that my younger sister was ill and that I was needed at home. So with a partial loss of summer income, I felt I would not be able to return to college that fall. But that was my limited, human thinking. God's thoughts are so much more positive and powerful than ours! Under his direction, I found myself back in school in September with a good off-campus part-time job in addition to the position of assistant to the

Dean of Women. This blessing covered my entire school bill for the final year. "Great is thy faithfulness!"… "Faithful is he who calleth you who also will do it" (I Thessalonians 5:24 KJV).

It was during my senior year that I was engaged to a ministerial student. Upon graduation, we were faced with another financial crossroad—whether to postpone our wedding in order to allow time for each of us to improve our depleted financial status or to proceed with our wedding plans and accept a home missionary pastorate with a small salary. We sought God's will together and concluded that we should exercise what Jesus Christ had taught; "But seek ye first the kingdom of God, and his righteousness; and all these things shall be added unto you" (Matthew 6:33 KJV); Our God honored his word to us in many ways.

We were one of three couples in the senior class that year who were being married just three weeks after graduation. The good news spread among the brides-to-be that there was a fantastic bridal gown sale at Hess Brothers, a large department store in Allentown, Pennsylvania. I saw a beautiful satin gown with an elegant train, exquisite lace and beaded trim. It was marked down half-price from $50, but that was still more than I could afford. Just a few days before my graduation, I made a final trip to the store's bridal department. Imagine my unbounded joy when the price tag had been lowered once again and this time to just $15! Someone loaned me a lovely veil, so my bridal outfit was a minimal expense. With a graduation gift, I was able to buy a pretty pink suit for our honeymoon trip.

As for household needs, it was just as if God had delegated a special crew to supervise getting us set up. After two pre-nuptial showers, the wedding reception, and two post-wedding receptions, we had such an abundance of household items that we could have practically opened a store with the surplus; all we lacked was a broom and an ironing board which we managed to get at an auction for just twenty-five cents. Friends donated used furniture which we

God Recycles **Broken** *Dreams*

enjoyed freshening up with paint or fabric. We bought a used refrigerator for just $20 and twelve years later sold it for $40. As we unpacked all our gifts in that cozy parsonage in Cherry Valley, New York, we literally wept for joy and gratitude to God for so many wonderful tokens of love from friends. God was true to his word again; He not only added all these things, but seemingly had multiplied them to us!

And that was just the beginning of innumerable financial and material blessings. When at the threshold of securing a teaching position in the public schools of California with a starting salary of about $10,000, I was offered a position at a Christian school during its struggling beginnings at a salary of $5,300. I went before the Lord with this proposition: "Father, it really doesn't matter to me which job you want me to accept, but if you want me in that Christian school at about half-salary of the public school, then you'll have to help me get everything at half-price."

And that's exactly what happened (remember the "half-price baby"!).

Just as God uses the wrath of man to praise him (Psalm 76:10), he also uses the mistakes of man to bless his children because I know I have been at the receiving end numerous times. Once Beverly and I were contemplating a trip and needed appropriate luggage. We went to a department store to browse, and as we got to the luggage department, my eyes caught sight of a beautiful three-piece set with lovely floral designs. It was presumptuous of me to even suggest, "Bev, if that set costs within the $25 range, we can get it."

Incidentally, I have learned that speaking forth and claiming something is practically tantamount to possessing it (Mark 11:23).

So as we approached the set I was really delighted to notice the price tag of $24.95. But in disbelief, I wondered if that price might apply just to one of the three pieces, so I sought out the clerk to ask. He seemed unsure… "We just got this set in today, so I really am not certain, but let me check with someone else."

In the meantime, I was talking secretly to my Father, "Please, Lord, let me have that beautiful set for $24.95."

I then heard the department head say to the clerk, "We can't seem to find the proper invoice for that set, so let the lady have it for that price."

To satisfy my curiosity, a few weeks later when I was in the same store again, I stopped by the luggage department and, sure enough, there was another beautiful set on display like the one I bought—but the price tag was $44.95!

Shopping for clothing can be a frustrating disaster or a rewarding adventure, depending whether or not we involve the Lord. I have tried it independently, and invariably I return home frazzled and exhausted and often disappointed with my purchase. But when I remember my Partner (Proverbs 3:5-6), he is honored, and consequently, I am blessed with serenity, joy and wonderful bargains. Also, I have learned the effective principle of spiritual agreement; whenever Bev and I go shopping together, we pray enroute for God's guidance to the right store and right prices. Whenever we forget to do this, our shopping is an utter catastrophe!

I needed a casual sports coat and noticed one on a discount rack at one of my favorite stores. Some deranged maniac had slashed (apparently with a razor blade) about twenty garments, including some fur coats. The gold corduroy coat, with a slash below the pocket, had been marked down from $23 to $14.25. Although that was a good reduction, I indicated to the clerk, "With such a sizeable slash, I really think this should have a bigger discount."

"I'll have to check with my supervisor, and she is not here this afternoon," she explained.

So I decided to talk to "my Supervisor" with this specific request, "Lord, when I come back on Friday, please let that coat be marked down to $10;" and as I left I "shot a prayer" at the coat—claiming it for that price. I am sure you have already guessed the rest of that story. Yes, on Friday, it was mine for

God Recycles **Broken** *Dreams*

$10! I truly felt sorry for the store management because of their loss, yet I was grateful to have benefitted from the "wrath of man."

It was a cold January evening when I was enroute to meet my brother-in-law, a teacher, and together we planned to attend a teachers' banquet in a famous Chinese restaurant in San Francisco. Wearing a long, black evening dress with just a light-weight shawl, I started talking to the Lord, "Father, I wish I could pick up a short white evening coat to wear tonight," and as I prayed, I even envisioned this white coat hanging on a rack in a certain department store just a few blocks off the freeway.

So I headed in that direction, and as I reached the store's coat department—there was a circular rack of "After Christmas Sale" white coats! Looking at the price tag, I was instantly filled with joy to realize I had the needed $25 (marked down from $49.95), which was Christmas gift money I had tucked away in my wallet.

"Do you want me to put it in a box or a bag?" The clerk asked.

"Oh neither, thank you, I believe I'll just wear it," I replied casually.

A precious P.S. to that episode was after I had met my brother-in-law, Wayne, with a happy explanation of my slight delay, we proceeded to the San Francisco Bay Bridge. Since he was driving his car, I offered my fifty cents for the bridge toll, but to our utter amazement, the clerk in the tollbooth smiled and said, "You go free... the people ahead of you handed me a dollar bill and told me to keep the change for the next car, so you're the lucky guy!"

About that time, the people ahead of us were looking back at us to catch our reaction. "Lord, sometimes you're too much!"

And it seems the more we convey our gratitude to our heavenly Father, just like an earthly parent whose children express their thanks, the more he loves to do for us!

I was admiring an adorable gold harp-designed clock (the very sight and sounds of harps are heavenly to me!). "Oh, Bev, would I ever like this clock for my birthday!" I exclaimed.

But the price tag of $28.95 was somewhat prohibitive. Upon examining it a little more closely, I noticed a slight scratch on the face. By that time the saleslady was inquiring, "May I help you?"

Almost without thinking I remarked, "This is adorable, but there's a flaw here. Maybe you'll sell it for half-price."

Really not serious about purchasing it, we started looking at some of the other fascinating clocks on display. Shortly, the saleslady came over to me and said, "The boss said you could have this for $14.50!"

"Thanks again, Lord. I really don't object being on this half-price salary and budget!"

Having moved from California to Florida and needing numerous household items in this new situation, again God graciously led me to half-price bargains in securing a desk, swivel chair, filing cabinet and lamps. At one furniture store, I noticed a colorful bedspread in bright orange, yellow, and green tones. It supported a sign—"Special Sale"—with a price tag of $25, marked down half price. These half-price items almost pursue me, it seems! As the saleslady was writing out the sales slip, she remarked, "I've had my eye on this pretty bedspread for a week, but I can't use it since it's a twin size."

Laughingly, I commented, "I'm sure glad you saw wrong, for it's full size!"

Then we both laughed, but I laughed last.

Leaving the furniture store, I was attracted to a little dress shop close by. Since our moving van had not arrived yet, we were in need of clothes hangers, so imagine my delight when I saw several stacks of hangers by the cash register, and only fifty cents for fifty. The joyful summation of this little shopping spree

God Recycles **Broken** *Dreams*

was that I had just received a gift of $14 in the mail the day before, and my newly purchased bedspread with the hangers, including the tax, totaled $13.99, leaving one cent as seed for the next shopping spree.

Besides envisioning what one hopes to get, speaking the word of confidence in God and agreeing in faith with someone, I have learned that the most productive joyful spiritual law of financial fulfillment is that of giving to the needs of others in obedience to God. Someone may say, "I already tithe, giving one-tenth of my income. What more does God want from me?"

Actually, tithing is just the beginning of giving. It opens the door to loving liberally. "The purpose of tithing is to teach you to always put God first in your lives" (Deuteronomy 14:23; also Malachi 3:10, Proverbs 3:9). It could be likened to a husband's giving his wife the expected grocery money from his paycheck and handing her an additional ten or twenty dollar bill, perhaps sacrificially, and saying lovingly, "Here, honey, get yourself something you've been wanting," this is the language of love—giving beyond what is expected.

Just so, our giving beyond our tithe is an expression of our love to God and his children. A byproduct of this whole process it that we, ourselves, are blessed with our own needs being met. The wise Solomon said, "It is possible to hold on too tightly and lose everything. Yes, the liberal man shall be rich! By watering others he waters himself" (Proverbs 11:24-25).

There are guidelines for both the rich and the poor in God's Word; "If God has given you money, be generous in helping others with it" (Romans 12:8b). And to the poorer, there is a caution as taught in the parable of Matthew 25:15-30 for that one who has the least not to hold on to it, but rather to invest even that smaller amount for the glory of God. It seems God usually taps me on the shoulder to help someone else when I feel I have the least to spare, and that can be scary. I gain inspiration every time I think of the widow of Zarephath, who was preparing her last meal for her son and herself. But when she gave it in faith and obedience to the prophet Elijah, her supply of flour and oil became inexhaustible. We are never losers when we give to God, for he will never be debtor to us.

While serving as principal of a Christian school, I was in a position to be aware of needs of faculty, students, and their families. Frequently, I had the joy of seeing my own limited income stretched to meet the needs of others. I remember one Saturday I took $6 worth of groceries to a needy family, and on the following Monday, I was handed an envelope with six dollars besides four packages of frozen meat—worth at least another $6. On another occasion I had received $20 in the mail from my brother, and with payday still a week away, I was really in need of it; but I felt prompted to give $10 of it to one of our staff members so he could take his wife out for their third wedding anniversary dinner. By evening of the same day, I was given a $15 honorarium for speaking in a church some weeks previously.

Richard, one of our fifth-grade students, had been working especially hard in a candy sale contest in order to win sufficient prize coupons to buy a camera. As it was nearing Christmas, he squelched his own desires so that he might select gifts from the coupon prize list for his parents, brother, and sister. Learning of his loving sacrifice, I felt I just must somehow secure a camera for him. But again, this was during a time of personal need, having just received two bills pertaining to my car that amounted to about $15. However, I scraped together the needed amount to purchase Richard a camera, and by the end of that week, our school treasurer approached me with an envelope saying, "Someone asked me to give this to you."—A check for $50!

"Thank you, 'somebody,' and thank you very much, Father."

So often God seems to return blessings in double measure… "She hath received of the Lord's hand double…" (Isaiah 40:2 KJV). I have experienced this sowing and reaping law of God's kingdom over and over again. For

God Recycles **Broken** *Dreams*

instance, once I felt I should give $20 to a prison ministry. Within a few days, a $20 gift came in the mail and another $20 for a speaking engagement. One outstanding "double blessing" was in the form of placemats. I had purchased a set of beautiful scenic mats, depicting the seasons with appropriate scriptures, at a church bazaar. Shortly after buying them, I realized it was nearing my friend Celia's birthday, and I just knew with her sensitive appreciation of the outdoors that these placemats would be the right gift for her. I struggled with that decision because I was unable to obtain another set for myself. Nevertheless, the set went to Celia. That was in October, and for Christmas, I received two sets of placemats as gifts—one, yes, was identical to the one I had given away and the second was even more beautiful with refreshing water scenes and also with Scripture inscriptions. I was doubly blessed!

So I have found my Lord to be very realistic in material needs and finances. He cares about college bills, bus fares, clothing, cameras, and placemats…and I still must tell you how he cared about a house, furniture, and a car! He even cares about a simple item like soap. I had occasion to share a cup of soap powder with a stranger in a laundromat who was traveling from out of town. The following week I was given a seven pound box of my favorite laundry soap powder!

God is good, and a good God likes to give, but we must get our thinking and doing in harmony with his laws of operation: namely, trust, obedience, and willingness to share with others as the Holy Spirit prompts us. This principle is taught in the Old Testament by Isaiah, "If you are willing and obedient, you shall eat the good of the land" (Chapter 1:19). Then, Jesus confirms it by saying, "For if you give, you will get! Your gift will return to you in full and overflowing measure, pressed down, shaken together to make room for more, and running over. Whatever measure you use to give—large or small—will be used to measure what is given back to you" (Luke 6:38).

"Father, I thank you that you have shown us by giving us your Son that love gives. May we, in turn, express our love to you and others by giving of ourselves and sharing what we have."

Chapter 7
So *This* Is Pastoring

We had just unpacked all our wedding gifts and arranged our used furniture in what seemed like a honeymoon cottage—but actually was a parsonage in the quiet town of Cherry Valley, New York. In such a romantic, seemingly ideal setting is where I was brought down to earth with a thud!

It was just the second monthly business meeting over which my husband presided in this our first pastorate. With the parsonage cottage directly attached to the church building in an L-shape, some of the business discussed traveled to the parsonage. In one particular session, there developed a heated debate as to which coal company to use for the winter's coal supply for the church and parsonage. Obviously losing his cool, a prominent member of the board went stalking out of the meeting with loud dissent.

Dear Lord! I prayed, is this what church work is all about? Is this what I've dreamed and prepared for all these years? Are churches made up of people like this?

After fourteen years of co-pastoring and fourteen additional years of being actively involved in church programs, I can say affirmatively, "Yes!" Churches are made up of people like this—people of flesh and blood—people in control and out of control—people with understanding and misunderstanding—people with maturity and immaturity.

But these are the very people who have given wealth of meaning and purpose to my life. My own spirit has been enriched and my heart enlarged through these many shared stressful and joyful experiences.

Who shares more intimately the joys and sorrows than the pastor and his wife? How well I remember walking together through the valley of the shadow of death with Ruth and Raymond—a most outstanding Christian couple in one of our pastorates. They had two fine, healthy sons of whom they were justly proud. Then a precious daughter was born, filling their hearts and home with even greater joy. But after a short season that joy turned into sorrow as they learned that little Mabel was afflicted with the usually fatal disease of the pancreas, cystic fibrosis. Because of much love and the best available medical care, this precious child did survive infancy and early childhood, but finally lost the battle after many brave struggles. In the meantime, a third son was born. Shortly after his birth, the mother said to me, "Ruth, I knew before I ever took Dean home from the hospital that he, too, showed symptoms of having the same illness as Mabel."

Indeed, his earthly life was very brief.

"Why do our children have to suffer like this? We love God, pray and tithe faithfully. What is God trying to tell us?"

They would agonizingly search for answers, and when with breaking hearts they had to give each of these precious young lives back to God, again they asked humbly, but honestly, "Why, God, must we give them up?"

At such times of sorrow, a pat answer like, "It must be God's will" does not comfort. I felt inspired, however, to share, "Ruth and Ray, God could not trust just anyone with such a sorrowful burden as you have carried these several years. He's not the Author of sorrow and sickness, but he has promised grace and strength to carry such a burden. Those who respond with trust and loving faithfulness to God through it all give witness to those who observe God's sustaining love and power. And what beautiful examples of God's grace you are!"

God Recycles **Broken** *Dreams*

Then there was that sorrow of watching cancer take a young husband and father of two small sons. An even greater sorrow was for us to learn that after we left that pastorate, this young widow allowed herself to become dissipated with unrestrained relationships. Her children had to be taken from her and placed in a foster home—fortunately of caring, Christian relatives.

These are some of the experiences that cause a minister to live close to the compassionate heart of the Great Shepherd. He will feel his heartbeat and convey his love and comfort to the needy ones.

As ministers of God's grace, we must be sensitive and alert to define God's character and ways from the misconceptions many have of God. For example, when a fine father was suddenly taken from his wife and three children by drowning in a scuba diving incident, I heard neighbors say accusingly, "I don't see how God could ever do a thing like this to such a wonderful family."

Even though I shared their hurt and sorrow, I was grateful I could clarify God's position with, "Our God did not cause or want this to happen. It was an accident. But when these tragedies do occur as part of living in this imperfect world, you can be assured that we have God's comfort and grace. Best of all, as we confess our faith in Him, we can be confident of eternal life, which means we can once again be reunited with our departed loved ones."

That seemed to be a key which opened up the passageway from my idealism to acceptable realism in dealing with people. The simple fact is that we are living in an imperfect world among imperfect people—including myself. Someone has aptly said, "If you should find a perfect church and then join it, it would no longer be perfect." Seriously, recognizing this simple truth with all its application has helped me to appreciate and enjoy people more and also to be more lenient with myself. It is too heavy a burden to be continually expecting perfection of others or of myself. To allow for mistakes and shortcomings is one of the sure cures for relief of tensions and frustrations inherently involved in human relations.

In this imperfect world, every minister encounters a diversified cross-section of human personalities, and our experiences were no exception. There was Millie—the smother mother whose darling daughter never received sufficient attention—at least according to her! We would receive periodic scathing phone calls, such as, "I can't understand why Sally was given the leading part in the Christmas program! She always seems to be out front. My Cindy was in tears when she came home tonight from the practice because she is only in the background angel choir."

Or another mother desirous of promoting her child's accomplishments would send a note, penned with hurtful pride, "I feel Nancy has been overlooked in being used for a piano solo in your special program. How can I encourage her to keep practicing when she's never given an opportunity to play!"

"Lord, how do we correct and console these distraught mothers? Oh, yes, I recall how you handled a mother who also was over-zealous in promoting her sons, James and John. In fact, she had the bold audacity to request the honored positions for her sons to sit right beside you in your kingdom! How ably you responded, 'Whoever would be great among you must be your servant, and whoever would be first among you must be your slave; even as the Son of man came not to be served, but to serve, and to give his life as a ransom for many'" (Matthew 20:20-28). "Thank you, Father, for allowing your Son to come down-to-earth to show us how to approach this problem. And like your Son, may we be examples teaching our parishioners the meaning of true humility!"

Not only were there the problems involving parents and their children, but the even more complex relationships between couples within a church family. There was the young wife who sought to get attention by accusing her husband of having an affair with the wife of another man within the church. Since both of the accused were active leaders of the youth group, the matter developed into a full-scale crisis, with members of the church taking sides.

God Recycles **Broken** Dreams

Realizing the gravity of this situation, I waited upon God in prayer and fasting, at which time he assured us, "Fear not, and be not dismayed at this great multitude; for the battle is not yours, but God's. You will not need to fight in this battle; take your position, stand still, and see the victory of the Lord on your behalf..." (II Chronicles 20:15, 17). In God's way and time the innocent youth leaders were exonerated, while the spirit of jealousy and dishonesty was exposed in the life of the accusing young wife. Her feigned fainting spells, together with her own instigated false witness letter were actually indictments against her. God's cleansing, healing love renewed relationships that had been injured in that whole stressful experience. "Oh, God, I'm so grateful for your hall of justice and mercy in which your Spirit of Truth exposes and declares true righteousness. Without him we fallible human beings would fail in our human relationships."

Perhaps one of the most disheartening burdens for a pastor is his concern for the unconcerned in his flock; those who are really not committed to Christ and his Kingdom. There again we find comfort in the fact that many of the professed followers of Jesus Christ himself during his earthly ministry were but emotional followers—as taught in his parable of the sower. He referred to those who at first received God's Word gladly, but as soon as problems and pressures came their way, they vanished. Then others allowed the cares of the world and their delight in riches to choke out God's Word in their lives. Then, thankfully, there are those who absorb the Word and reproduce (Matthew 13). At one point in Jesus' ministry when the cost of true discipleship was revealed, it is recorded that "Many of his disciples went back and walked no more with Him." Jesus then pressed his remaining twelve, "Will you also go away?" (John 6:66-68). "So, Jesus, at least you understand the pain and loss of having followers coming and going."

In pastoral work, as in the world of nature, it is not all cloudy weather, storms and valleys; there are also many moments of bright sunshine, balmy breezes and joyous mountaintops. What a privilege to be invited to celebrate not only high moments of parishioners' joyous ecstasy, but also those little everyday blessings. How true it is: "To share a joy, makes it double; to share a sorrow, lessens the trouble." To officiate at weddings of the young couples, whom we loved and taught the ways of God, was always a high moment of joy. Isn't it good to realize that Jesus Christ and his disciples were invited guests at a wedding! (John 2:1-12). In fact, that event records his first miracle. Perhaps if more couples would invite Jesus Christ to be the guest of honor at their wedding, they, too, would experience miracles of his presence and power; then later share the joy of welcoming a precious baby in dedication to God—this always was a holy privilege.

There were those innumerable pleasantries of being invited to take a ride in a parishioner's new car (I'll never forget that bright new yellow and black Buick), or of a frightening trip aboard another's new yacht; or down the dark shaft of a member's coal mine, or to walk about in another's fruitful fields and then to be loaded down with vine-ripened vegetables in such bountiful supply that we would fill several hundred quarts of canned goods during harvest time. To enter into the joys of Jack's successful business venture, Bob and Ethel's home renovation, Jimmy's high school honors; to be the recipient of the ladies' sewing circle's colorful autographed quilt, and to receive armloads of groceries at those old-fashioned Pennsylvania Dutch "poundings for the pastor," and the innumerable tokens of love at special seasons of the year—How can one possibly be deserving of these many kindnesses!

How can I ever forget dear Mrs. Hoover, owner of the small corner grocery store just across from our parsonage, who invariably every Saturday evening would come across the street and present us with a package of meat for our Sunday dinner. Also, she handed us an envelope of carefully accumulated shiny quarters and half-dollars; "I always like to give my Lord the best," she would say humbly.

God Recycles **Broken** *Dreams*

The Bible does teach that "those who are taught the Word of God should help their teachers by paying them" (Galatians 6:6). And Paul urged, "But we beseech you, brethren, to respect those who labor among you and are over you in the Lord and admonish you to esteem them very highly in love because of their work" (I Thessalonians 5:12-13 KJV). Our parishioners often gave of themselves, their time, and material possessions to bless our lives; it is both rewarding and humbling to be a servant of the Lord!

Although all these material tokens of love bring joy to the heart of a pastor, there is no greater joy than that of realizing one has been an instrument of God's peace and pardon to a guilt-ridden heart. The Word teaches that God "...hath given us the ministry of reconciliation" (II Corinthians 5:18 KJV). We have the privilege of bringing together God and man!

I will always cherish that memorable day when Harry, the town drunkard, came stumbling to our parsonage door, desperately crying out for a change of life. "Reverend," he pled with my husband, "I just can't go on this way. My wife is threatening to leave me, and I know I've been a miserable husband and father. Can you help me?"

"I know One who can!" my husband assured him, "but Harry, are you really willing to forsake this way of living and allow Jesus Christ to be Lord of your life and home?"

He admitted that he was and, humbly confessing his sinful ways to God and trusting the Savior for forgiveness, Harry truly became "... a new creature in Christ Jesus."

Experiencing the burst of this new life in Christ, Harry urged my husband, "Would you go with me to visit my buddy Joe... he's had a drinking problem just like me and is in bad shape."

So within minutes, my husband and transformed Harry were met at the door of Joe's home. Actually, before they had knocked, they had heard the raging cursings of Joe against his meek wife. Catching a glimpse of Harry's radiant countenance, Joe exclaimed, "Whatever has happened to you, Harry!"

"I've got religion, Joe," Harry announced, "and I want you to have it, too. It's really wonderful!"

After explaining the new birth through repentance and faith in Jesus Christ, my husband also led Joe into a new life in Christ. This was a joint celebration in heaven and earth, for truly, "... there is joy in the presence of the angels of God over one sinner that repenteth" (Luke 15:10 KJV). The sequel to that event was Joe's passing just a few months after his confession of Christ as Savior.

Then there was Helen, a devout follower of Greek Orthodoxy, who had had a very meaningful dream. In this dream, she saw her mother-in-law who had died some years previously reaching down to her and encouraging her, "Helen, don't you think it is time for you to get ready for eternity?"

Just as she was pondering this dream, my husband happened to arrive at her door for a pastoral visit. She was ready to learn about salvation and to become a believer in Jesus Christ.

These transformed lives were just the beginning of many more who were led to Christ Jesus. At one pastorate, especially, there were many young couples with their children who confessed Christ as Savior. That particular congregation had been stifled by legalistic preaching by our predecessors and, consequently, searching hearts were kept out of the kingdom of God. We learned through painful experiences that often denominational leaders take the role of the biblical Pharisees, and as Jesus described, "They load you with impossible demands that they themselves don't even try to keep" (Matthew 23:4). And, "You ignore God's specific orders and substitute your own traditions. You are simply rejecting God's laws and trampling them under your feet for the sake of tradition" (Mark 7:8-9). This is the sad plight of many present-day congregations that live under the deathly threat of man-made rules rather than thriving under the life-giving flow of the Holy Spirit.

God Recycles **Broken** *Dreams*

At this pastorate where spiritual death had taken its toll, we faithfully sowed the seed of God's Word not only in the Sunday services but also during the week in home Bible studies, youth groups, children's Bible Clubs and ladies' share and prayer times. After a year of scattering this life-giving seed, we were overjoyed with an abundant harvest of many transformed lives and homes in that community. Jesus said, "The truth shall make you free…" (John 8:32 KJV).

At the end of that conference year, the presiding district superintendent, as part of his annual report to the conference delegates, gave a glowing report of this revived and growing parish. Rather than absorb the praise that was given to us personally, we acknowledged this phenomenal spiritual harvest to be the result of teaching God's Word in truth—a contrast to using it as a weapon of death. "… The letter killeth, but the Spirit giveth life" (II Corinthians 3:6 KJV).

How devastating it was to us and to this vibrant congregation when a change took place in the leadership of that district which smacked of Pharisaical legalism again, with all the "… Thou shalt not wear… Thou shalt not go… Thou shalt not do…" On one occasion my husband was censored by the district council for having worn Bermuda shorts while mowing the parsonage lawn—what a sad commentary on the leaders' priorities! Unable to minister within these restrictions, we sadly resigned.

I will never forget the evening we left that community where our hearts had become so closely knit together in God's love. We drove slowly down one of the main streets leading out of town, when suddenly we were aware of someone running alongside our car, desperately trying to get our attention. We looked out, and there was Jerry, another town drunk whose life we had touched with God's love. "Preacher," he muttered falteringly, "I just want to wish you the best of luck and to thank you for all you've done for us."

With tear-filled eyes we were reminded how Jesus also had been loved and welcomed by the publicans and sinners but quite often rejected by the religious leaders. He was even chased out of the synagogues (Luke 4). *I'm glad you understand, Jesus, how we feel!*

Some view the life of a pastor as an easy way of life—just preaching two sermons on Sunday, giving a Bible study on Wednesday evening, visiting the sick and drawing a salary. But quite the contrary, ministers have a heavy assignment expending spiritual, emotional, and mental energy. Studies have been made that have revealed preaching a one-hour sermon consumes as much physical energy as eight hours of hard manual labor. A pastor punches no time clock, but like the old-fashioned country doctor, he is "on call" from early morning until late at night and even during the night if needed. Like other public figures, he is expected to smile, listen, and offer a cheerful word no matter what.

Oftentimes, a congregation forgets to take into account that this heavily-burdened pastor also carries many burdens of his own. There are financial stresses, medical bills, car repairs, emotional fatigue, loneliness, and unjust criticisms—all seem to be part of the price tag of leadership. How good it would be if a congregation developed a keener listening ear and understanding heart for its pastor's needs. Why can't there be a *mutual* ministry of love between pastor and laity? Praise God for the parishioners who are sensitive to their pastor's needs. We read of the women who followed and ministered to the needs of Jesus (Luke 23:49), and also Paul refers in various epistles to those who stood by and strengthened him. It would serve the laity well to remember that as they minister to their pastor's needs, they share in the rewards of his spiritual harvest (Matthew 10:41-42).

A pastoral family has frequent challenges and adjustments to make in fulfilling God's call on their lives. In many instances, there is no choice in the matter of living quarters—that has been predetermined by the permanent church parsonage; this can be good or bad, depending upon upkeep of the house.

God Recycles **Broken** *Dreams*

How well I remember, while considering accepting a pastorate in Pennsylvania, being shown a one-room schoolhouse the church had bought and planned to convert into the parsonage. Being young and adventurous, we accepted the challenge of living temporarily with one electrical outlet, running water if I would run for it—up to the source at the adjoining campground—and the infamous His and Her bathrooms (air-conditioned, of course!) But after many months of hard work, my husband transformed that barren schoolhouse into an incredibly attractive eight-room house, including a heating system (which had involved digging out a basement), a cozy kitchen and dining room, a beautiful bathroom, a 14′ x 30′ living room, and three bedrooms. That congregation was doubly blessed to have a preacher and a builder.

Aside from the adjustments to new communities, cultures and housing, there are often unwritten, but nevertheless exacting, demands and expectations on a minister's wife and family to be ideal (some would say "perfect"). How many minister's children have rightfully resented the requirements of being a PK (Preacher's Kid). Why can't the minister's family be accepted as flesh and blood, normal people just as the minister must accept his parishioners? This Christian courtesy would alleviate much destructive criticism and needless pain in the parsonage and possibly even keep many PKs from turning their backs on God and the church. I am reminded of a fine pastor whose daughter became pregnant out of wedlock, and consequently, the church congregation dismissed this pastor and his family. I can hear those pious Pharisees now: *We must keep our religious skirts clean. This is hard on our reputation—so be gone!*

How redemptive it would have been for that congregation to have ministered compassion and love to this distraught pastor and his wife *and* forgiveness to their daughter. Speaking of a pastor's burdens and frustrations, perhaps one of the most debilitating is that of having his leadership challenged with smug complacency, as in: *We've always done it this way, so why change now?*

What is more traditionally root-bound than religion? Religiosity can be a hindrance to growing faith in the Savior. Truth is eternal. It never changes, but the methods and applications often do.

On numerous occasions, we were unduly criticized for trying to make the gospel relevant to the needs of our present age and location in which we served. At one midweek service, a Pennsylvania Dutchman felt he had to vent his disapproval of our taking leadership in a community choir. He thought "they" were a worldly group of people, stating that Jesus says to come out from among them and be separate. My husband responded succinctly that Jesus taught *insulation*—not *isolation*.

It was often a matter of trying to serve "new wine" in "old wineskins," which Jesus admittedly said just would not work. Trying to use new ways often just burst the old wineskins with the pressure of change. Jesus taught, "Only new wineskins are used to store new wine: That way both are preserved" (Matthew 9:16-17).

So, this is pastoring—joys and sorrows, ups and downs, criticisms and rewards. Is it worth it? I must disclose that these experiences took their tragic toll upon my disheartened husband. So he would have to answer in the negative: "No it wasn't worth it."

He does not stand alone—or fall alone—many a minister has succumbed under the pressures and demands of his calling. Even as Jesus Christ was crucified by the religious leaders of his day, so these dedicated ministers are often emotionally and spiritually crucified by either the pharisaical hierarchy of denominations or by the local church leaders.

In contrast, and with no "holier-than-thou" attitude, my answer to "Is it worth it?" is an emphatic, whole-hearted "Yes!" In spite of all its imperfections, the church of Jesus Christ will always have my love and loyalty, for it is in the framework of the church that I have found and shared the Pearl of

God Recycles **Broken** *Dreams*

Great Price, and when one finds Him, nothing else really matters that much! (Matthew 13:45-46).

The following is a farewell tribute to us from the dear mother whose two young children preceded her in death.

Our Pastor and His Wife

Our pastor is small in stature
But has a voice so deeply toned;
He used to preach the Gospel
To poor and needy souls.

He played his guitar and trombone
And sang many a pretty song,
To help cheer the weary pilgrims,
To keep on traveling along.

He visited the sick and weary,
Both men, women, and children alike.
He didn't show partiality,
And that is what everyone liked.

He may not have pleased all the people,
But I'm sure he meant everything well.
He remodeled the parsonage so beautifully
For him and his wife to dwell.

He has a sweet wife to help him,
To bear all the burdens of life,
Together they walk life's pathways
And help to influence us right.

She played the piano so talented,
And taught music lessons here and there,
The children learned very nicely,
To display their talents elsewhere.

She took pastries and all kind of goodies
To cheer people up when distressed,
I am sure she will be rewarded in Heaven
Among God's honored and blessed.

She was a good Sunday School teacher,
Who taught the lessons quite well,
And to find her tardy even one Sunday
Would be very hard to tell.

As they labored together so nicely,
In the little white church in Lavelle,
The fellowship we shared together
Shall always in our memories dwell.

"Oh, Father God—our great Shepherd—please strengthen and bless every true shepherd, especially the discouraged and disheartened ones. And may the sheep be sensitive followers."

God Recycles **Broken** *Dreams*

Chapter 8
Edge of Eternity

Although there is but a thin, invisible veil between the earthly and the heavenly, between the mortal and the eternal, yet it seems so much of our living demands our preoccupation with the earthly—working, sleeping, eating, and caring for the basic needs of life. So it is really in God's grace when we find ourselves in circumstances that jolt us loose from the confines of earth into a new focus of eternity. I have had several such experiences that will forever satisfy my mind that there is eternal life after death, that the invisible hosts of angels are as real as our visible friends, and that eternal values transcend the earthly.

How well I recall the evening when the dean of the women's dorm knocked at my door to inform me, "Ruth, you are wanted on the phone... it's a long distance call."

Immediately, my thoughts flew to my dear father, just forty-seven years of age at the time, who was being hospitalized in my home town of Schenectady, New York. The latest word I had received from Mother said the doctors still were in a quandary as to what was causing the swelling in his joints and the pain in his lower back.

"I hope Daddy hasn't worsened," was my first frightened concern. Hastening to the phone booth, I heard my mother's voice on the other end of the line, and by the worried tone of her voice I sensed immediately the gravity of the situation.

"Ruthie," Mother requested, "I need you to come home… Dad isn't doing well."

I assured Mother I would make arrangements to get home as soon as possible. Hanging up the phone, all my pent-up fears burst out into a flood of tears. "Oh, God," I pled, "please don't let anything happen to my precious Daddy!"

Then I reminded God of that evening when, while in prayer, I had sensed a special moment of faith to believe for his healing and upon later inquiry, I learned that Dad, at that very hour and several hundred miles away, had experienced an unusual power and presence of God surging through his body; he said it had seemed like divine electric currents sweeping through his body. So I had taken that as a token of God's healing my father, and even though his condition worsened, I clung to that assurance.

"But now, Lord, what does this call from home mean… please, God, let him get well again."

As I started back to my dorm room, I was stopped in my tracks! I heard the sound of voices in song coming from the girls' lounge on the first floor. They had gathered there that evening for a joint time of devotions, and now they were singing so appropriately,

> "He will give me grace and glory,
> He will give me grace and glory,
> He will give me grace and glory,
> And go with me, with me all the way." E.W. Blandy

"Oh, Father," I thought with an aching heart, "If you go with me and give me your grace and glory, I believe I can make it."

When I arrived home, I was painfully shocked to see how ill my father looked as he lay in the hospital bed. After more diagnostic and exploratory

God Recycles **Broken** *Dreams*

tests, the doctors' solemn verdict was that our dad had cancer—and in such an advanced stage as to be inoperable.

Not having adequate hospitalization coverage, together with the fact that we desired to give our dad all the loving care he deserved, we decided to have him released from the hospital and brought home by ambulance. Since we could not afford a full-time nurse, it became my duty to assist Mother in caring for him. Sleeping across the hallway from his room, I would listen for his restlessness and groans of discomfort and then get up to administer pain shots for relief. Dad was such a patient sufferer and always so grateful for any kindness shown to him; even in his weakest moments, he would whisper "Thank you."

The walls of his bedroom were soon covered with greeting cards from his many friends who were praying for him and wishing him well. Even a rather ungodly group of fellow workers who had mocked him on many occasions for his faith in God now came in this sobering hour to give him a substantial gift of money to help defray medical expenses, and they let it be known how much they truly admired him.

Each morning after I had freshened Dad's room, he would ask me to share a promise out of God's Word with him, and then we would have prayer together. As a tumor developed on his brain, his thinking and memory processes were affected; yet whenever he shared with friends or family concerning eternal matters—his hope of eternal life—his peace and joy in Christ his Lord—then his thoughts and words were completely clear and true. Often Dad would ask me to go downstairs to play some of his favorite hymns on the piano such as "Amazing Grace," "What a Friend We Have in Jesus," "Take the Name of Jesus with You," and "The Lily of the Valley."

It was one of those times when Dad had requested some songs that I asked, "What would you like me to play, Daddy?"

"Oh, some hymns about heaven."

So I scurried down the stairs and started playing a medley of all the songs I knew Dad loved on the theme of heaven, including, "In the Sweet By and By," "When We All Get to Heaven," "In the New Jerusalem," and "Zion's Hill."

In the midst of this, I became suddenly aware of something strangely beautiful taking place upstairs. I ceased my playing, tiptoed softly upstairs and sat quietly on my bed. With Mother at his bedside, Dad was in an almost sacred conversation with his eternal God. I felt I must record what he was saying in my diary: "Heavenly Father, how I love you and praise you. Now I give Sammy into your hands. Take care of Violet and Ruthie and Esther and Marvin (the five of us children). And take Machen's hand." (This was his pet name for my mother, Magdalen).

Then he would pause and he seemed to be at the very threshold of heaven itself. It was almost as if he had caught a glimpse of eternal light, to which he responded, "Oh, streams of glory are flooding my soul... Praise the Lord! Praise the Lord!"

Then there was a holy hush and finally one more release and request, "And now, heavenly Father, take me... hold my hand." Truly this deeply moving experience took place at the edge of eternity!

For the next three days as Dad lay in a coma, we three older children took turns staying by his bedside. Not having experienced death in our immediate family before this, I was dreading the unknown intruder. But that evening of March 23 when Violet sensed a change had taken place, we quickly gathered around our precious father as he breathed his last breath. The weary pilgrim had arrived at his eternal home. For the first time in my life, I was aware of the presence of angels. I was so conscious of their holy hushed movements pervading that humble bedroom that all my fears and dread of death were replaced with a deep sense of peace. These angels had come to escort my father to his eternal abode—in the very presence of God!

God Recycles **Broken** *Dreams*

Of course, I suffered the indescribable sorrow and pain of our human separation, but as I was reminded by God's promise that we would be reunited again, the sorrow gradually diminished. Let me share that hope with you: "I want you to know what happens to a Christian when he dies so that when it happens, you will not be full of sorrow, as those who have no hope. When Jesus returns, God will bring back with him all the Christians who have died. And the believers who are dead will be the first to rise to meet the Lord. Then we who are still alive and remain on the earth will be caught up with them in the clouds to meet the Lord in the air and remain with him forever" (I Thessalonians 4:13-14, 16-17).

I must say my faith took quite a setback when my Dad was not healed—especially since we had had that mutual experience of God's presence, which we had interpreted as a token of God's healing. I struggled with that deeply disappointing trauma until finally, God, through his faithful Holy Spirit, seemingly whispered into my "inner ear," "Your father is completely whole—healed in the truest sense in the presence of his Lord." That was another peek into eternity!

In the second year of our marriage, I experienced another extraordinary sorrow: As any normal couple expecting their first child, my husband and I were so full of joyful expectations that this new, yet unborn member of our family seemed to be the favorite topic of our conversation. We had so many thoughts and plans for this unseen life! Having been the recipient of two lovely baby showers, I had drawers and boxes full of all kinds of darling infant garments and accessories. The borrowed bassinet was ready and colorful rattles decorated the baby's dresser.

On the Sunday evening before the labor began, I was in a church service where some friends presented me with a huge basket of the most colorful assortment of hybrid gladiolus I had ever seen. As I received them gladly (how else when they were gladiolus!), I said prophetically to my friends, "I'll probably be taking these with me to the hospital tomorrow."

Sure enough, by early next morning, I was at the hospital in labor. But as the hours stretched into seemingly unending agony, I sensed something was wrong. Finally, when the relief of birth came, I was dreadfully aware of the deadly silence of the attendant doctor and nurses… and especially the absence of that first healthy cry of a newborn infant. In a matter-of-fact tone, the doctor broke the silence with, "Mrs. Shank, your baby is a boy, but something went wrong. He's not alive."

Almost too weak to weep, my spirit ached with an inexpressible hurt. I will never forget the cold callousness of one of the attending nurses who tried to dispel the disappointment of nine months' expectations with a flippant, "Well, those things just happen sometimes, Mrs. Shank!"

Within minutes my husband was at my side with the shock of disbelief upon his countenance; we sorrowed together silently. Also God had arranged to have my former roommate from college, Esther Merrill, on vacation from Indiana, to be with us just when we needed that extra support. Like Esther in the Bible, she had come "… for such a time as this."

After having wheeled me into my room, a nurse brought this precious infant wrapped in a blanket for us to see. He had been a beautifully formed, full-term baby boy with a round face and lots of black hair, but there was no life. As I glanced over at the basket of lovely gladiolus that had gladdened my heart just 24 hours before—now they seemed to take the form of funeral flowers, and my heart grieved. Instead of receiving congratulatory cards, we received sympathy cards. It was almost more than I could bear!

What added to my already aching heart were such messages from well-meaning, but in error, Christians as, "May it comfort your hearts to realize that this disappointment was in God's will."

I wrestled with that concept with an honest hurting heart, "Could our heavenly Father, who loves us and loves babies, give us a dead baby?" The answer

God Recycles **Broken** *Dreams*

came through in a most unexpected, but assuring way that very first night after the initial sorrow.

Having fallen asleep from sheer physical and emotional exhaustion, I was abruptly awakened by the cries of the newborn infants in the hospital nursery, which unfortunately was located within hearing distance of my room. Upon awakening so suddenly, my thoughts were in a flurry of confusion. "Oh, I finally had our baby," was my first realization as I felt my deflated abdomen. Trying to recollect the happening of the previous day, I thought, "The doctor said we had a boy." But then in a split second the reality of the words, "… but something went wrong… he's not alive," hit me with full impact. "This just can't be," I thought, "we've been talking and waiting and feeling this new life for nine months. I must have my baby." But as I heard the nurses' footsteps delivering babies to their respective mothers for the midnight feeding—I was bypassed.

With my heart breaking and tears streaming down my face in torrents, I suddenly became aware of the presence of a host of angelic beings; my room was full of them, and they were singing:

> "He knows it all—
> Your tears—how fast they fall;
> Your Father knows,
> He knows it all."

As they sang, it was as if billows of peace swept over my troubled spirit.

In that moment, I realized that my heavenly Father and my Lord Jesus Christ were sorrowing with me. Even as Jesus Christ had sorrowed with the widow whose son had died and had wept at the death of his friend Lazarus, he was now touched by my grief. My God had not planned this disappointment for us; it was not part of God's will for us to have a dead baby, but rather this was part of the curse on the human family. Since we were members of that human family, we could not escape its many sorrows. But now in the midst of this sorrow, my heavenly Father was compassionately sharing our sorrow—what comfort and relief these messengers of God brought to my breaking heart that night. "Are they not all ministering spirits, sent forth to minister for them who shall be heirs of salvation" (Hebrews 1:14 KJV). "…God, my maker, who giveth songs in the night" (Job 35:10 KJV). "… In the night, his song shall be with me, and my prayer unto the God of my life" (Psalm 42:8 KJV). Yes, I know God gives songs in the night—I heard them—and by heavenly hosts!

One of the benefits of sorrow, besides the needful and glorious glimpses into eternity, is that we can more fully empathize with others who sorrow. Within the same year that we had our stillborn infant, we learned of another minister couple whose first baby also was stillborn. I was told by a mutual friend that Lucille was grieving so deeply that she had withdrawn from her friends and church; somehow she was unable to lift the shades of gloom. Having experienced the same trauma, and having received the healing comfort of the Holy Spirit, I was able to write a letter to Lucille and Frank that was from my heart to theirs. Some weeks later, I learned that God had used this letter to lift the cloud of despair that had settled upon Lucille's life. Aren't we taught by Paul, "Blessed be God… the God of all comfort; who comforteth us in all our tribulation, that we may be able to comfort them which are in any trouble, that we may be able to comfort wherewith we ourselves are comforted of God" (II Corinthians 1:4 KJV).

Not only in times of death but also in the times of illness God often peels off the earthly cataracts from our eyes so that we might gain new perspectives with eternal significance. During my principalship of El Sobrante Christian School, there were several occasions when I landed in the hospital because of the overload. I can recall in one such circumstance, looking up to God and almost accusingly saying, "Lord, I just *can't* be here. Don't you realize this is the opening of school, and I'm needed in my office?"

God Recycles **Broken** *Dreams*

Without any hesitation or apology, the Holy Spirit seemed to flash on the screen of my mind in blazed letters, "*HE MAKETH ME TO LIE DOWN!*" For a moment I had to debate with myself if that strong word could have come out of the well-loved 23rd Psalm, but indeed it had! God had to remind me while lying there immobile that just as when an electric circuit was overloaded, it would blow a fuse for safety, so whenever I allowed my physical and emotional systems to become overtaxed, there would be a breakdown—and for my own protection.

There are innumerable lessons God would teach us through our illnesses (and not with an accusing finger or condemning tone of voice), and I truly feel persuaded that many prayers for healing are being unanswered pending our first listening and learning what God would teach us. Didn't Jesus Christ, the very Son of God, have to learn obedience by the things he suffered (Hebrews 5:8)?

Often during times of illness, we add a needless burden of guilt to our already burdened body by assuming God is punishing us for some misdeed or failure of the past. Would a true, loving earthly father punish his child with sickness? How absurd! Then why do we accuse our heavenly Father of such a misdeed? My own godly brother, Sam, endured for 20 years in the valley of suffering—not only physically as a result of very critical and debilitating brain surgery—but also emotionally and spiritually, because unfortunately there are still some of Job's "comforters" around who tried to persuade Sam that his physical problem must somehow bespeak God's disapproval of his imperfect Christian walk.

In a letter from Sam, he shared, "I am particularly grateful for your real note of compassion. It is very hard to handle my heavy loss (loss of balance in walking, muscle control, and hampered vision), and it is much harder when my loved ones conclude that because of my many misdeeds, God's hand is so heavy upon me."

This seems to be an age-old approach to suffering—to blame either God or the sufferer because of some sin in his life. To blame God is absurd because all that sickness implies—deterioration and death—is in sharp contrast to the very nature of God, which is life and wholeness. There certainly are instances where one has abused his body and then must suffer the consequences; I learned recently of a thirty-two-year-old wife who died of lung cancer. That seems to us an untimely death, but she had smoked profusely and this was a consequence. There are many other instances, though, of sickness which are not the result of the sufferer's sin. The disciples questioned Jesus concerning the man born blind, "Was it a result of his own sins or those of his parents?" To which Jesus replied, "Neither, but to demonstrate the power of God" (John 9:1-3).

From the Christian viewpoint, I feel scripture would teach us that primarily Satan is the source of sickness—whether in direct attacks, as illustrated in the case of Job, or indirectly through his having injected the human race with his venom, which is expressed in viruses and an unending list of diseases. We must resist Satan (James 4:8, I Peter 5:9, Luke 10:19) and overcome him through the power of Jesus Christ. Yet the fact remains that some choice children of God are not healed on earth and this is no reflection on their lack of faith, but rather an indication that we are not yet fully freed from the curse of Satan. However, that day will come: "Yet what we suffer now is nothing compared to the glory he will give us later. For all creation is waiting patiently and hopefully for that future day when God will resurrect his children. For on that day thorns and thistles, sin, death, and decay will all disappear, and the world around us will share in the glorious freedom from sin which God's children enjoy." For we know that even the things of nature, like animals and plants, suffer in sickness and death as they await this great event. And *even we Christians*, although we have the Holy Spirit within us as a foretaste of future glory, also groan to be released from pain and suffering. We, too, wait anxiously for that day when God will give us our full rights as

God Recycles **Broken** *Dreams*

his children, including the new bodies he has promised us—bodies that will never be sick again and will never die" (Romans 8:18-23).

Although Satan is the primary cause of sickness, I feel we must honestly face up to the fact that we can bring on illnesses by our own negative thinking and living. The wise Solomon wrote, "A cheerful heart does good like medicine, but a broken spirit makes one sick" (Proverbs 17:22). Also John gives us the thought-provoking wish, "Beloved, I wish above all things that thou mayest prosper and be in health, even as thy soul prospereth" (III John 2 KJV). If our soul, which includes our emotions, intellect and will, chooses the path of *dis-ease*, the inevitable result is disease. On the other hand, if we *choose* to think and feel "... what is true and good and right, pure and lovely, and dwell on the fine, good things in others, and think about all you can praise God for and be glad about" (Philippians 4:8), then we have God's peace within, which affects the body without.

Not only can negative thinking and living harm us physically, but also our careless breaking of God's physical laws—and let him who is innocent, cast the first stone. (I don't hear many thuds!) When we overeat or eat harmful foods (and one wonders if there are many truly beneficial foods available in this age of chemical sprays, fertilizers and preservatives), our bodies express their revulsion in sickness. When we short-change ourselves in rest, our resistance is weakened, and we open the door to an invasion of germs. When we fail to exercise properly, like an unused piece of machinery, we become sluggish and weak. All this can be summed up in the desire of the Psalmist, "You have made my body, Lord; now give me sense to heed your laws" (Psalm 119:73). Also, we have food for thought in Psalm 103:5 KJV, "Who satisfieth thy mouth with good things; so that thy youth is renewed like the eagles."

So, it would seem to me that the source of our illnesses is two-fold—either from Satan or from our own negligence, but never from God as a punishment. But what can we do for relief when sickness strikes? There are times God heals directly and miraculously; there are times He heals through the hands and skill of doctors; there are times he heals through a natural process of the body's own restorative powers or in a curative climate; also, by our getting in harmony with God's natural laws. "Keep these thoughts ever in mind; let them penetrate deep within your heart, for they will mean real life for you, and radiant health" (Proverbs 4:23).

Perhaps the greatest test of faith is when one is ill, and regardless of cause or cures tried, the condition remains or gets worse. God can use such experiences, if allowed, to purify us and to strengthen our grip on eternal life. "The bodies we have now embarrass us, for they become sick and die; but they will be full of glory when we come back to life again. Yes, they are weak, dying bodies now, but when we live again they will be full of strength" (I Corinthians 15:43). When we are set aside from the racetrack of life, we have a unique opportunity to re-evaluate where we are going and what we are going after, to separate the fleeting from the permanent, the earthly from the eternal. We all need times of sorting out our priorities in the light of eternity.

So even though God is not the author of sickness, and he is not trying to punish us or get even with us, yet he can use that for our growth and maturity (I Peter 4:1-2). Regardless of what comes enroute from earth to glory, we must believe, "*ALL* things work together for good to them that love God" (Romans 8:28 KJV)… Either God is true or a liar, but "… Let God be true and every man a liar…" (Romans 3:4 KJV).

I would like to share one more experience at the edge of eternity which occurred when my precious Mother was called home to be with her Lord.

It was very early on a December Sunday morning that I awakened from a dream which I felt had some special significance. I dreamed that my mother, my brother Sam and I were sitting around a small table in a dimly lit room eating large berries from a common bowl. As I pondered this dream, I felt perhaps it symbolized our fellowship in suffering in that my brother was very ill at that particular time. But later in that same day, I received a phone call from my sister, Esther, saying our Mother had graduated to her heavenly home during the night.

When I had left California months previously to answer God's call to move to Florida, I wondered as I kissed Mother farewell if I would see her again on this earth because she was eighty-one years of age and showing signs of weakening. Yet for her years she still maintained quite an active interest in her church, especially in the Ladies' Bible Class. Also, she was frequently found in her kitchen baking all kinds of German pastries, kuchen and cookies that she freely gave to neighbor children, the groceryman, mailman and anyone she felt needed a little "pick-me-up."

But one could find Mother most frequently in her favorite armchair listening to her much-loved Christian TV or radio programs, or else just sitting there quietly in meditation and prayer. Her prayer list had no boundaries and was lifted to the Lord many times in the day and even night hours when sleep eluded her. It was in this very armchair that dear Mother just fell asleep in the arms of Jesus. She had been grocery shopping that day with Esther but had complained of feeling so very tired. Esther brought Mother home, carried in her groceries and then went back to continue some shopping, including the purchase of an extraordinarily beautiful poinsettia plant for Mother's Christmas holiday season.

But Mother never saw that lovely gift because when Esther went to her door early Sunday morning to present the plant to her, she observed the strangeness of all the drapes still closed. So getting her husband, Wayne, to enter Mother's house with her, her apprehensions were realized—Mother had never gone to bed that Saturday night. Her bedspread had been thrown back in readiness, and she had curlers in her hair in preparation for Sunday best. Instead, she had been taken to her eternal rest.

This was a sweet sorrow to us—sweet because of her peaceful homegoing—but sorrowful because of the human separation. My sorrow was compounded because of my inability to attend Mother's memorial service, which consisted of a graveside committal service, followed by a Celebration of Eternal Life in the church which was attended by her many friends. However, even though circumstances prohibited my presence at the memorial service, I was inspired to write a poem which was read there in my absence. Since "Silent Night" was Mother's favorite carol from Germany, it was appropriate to us that this be the theme of her memorial service:

Silent Night—Holy Night

It was a "Silent Night—Holy Night"

When our precious Mother fell asleep in Christ,

While sitting in her living room chair-

Surely angels were hovering there!

This had been her favorite place

From which she had sought the Throne of Grace;

Interceding, with tears of praise and love,

Lifting family and friends to God above.

So this was a very holy night (December 3, 1977)

When God sent his angels on a special flight

To escort dear Mother thru the gates of heaven,

Into the Presence of her Lord, for whom she'd been living.

Her last day on earth was a Saturday,

Grocery shopping with plans to bake and give away,

For along with concern and prayer for others-

Putting together "care packages"—that was our Mother!

God Recycles **Broken** *Dreams*

As evening drew near, there were plans for tomorrow;

With curlers in her hair, purse and shoes in a row,

Her bedspread thrown back, but no need to lie down,

For her Sabbath would be in heaven, and on her head, a golden crown.

On her dining room table lay a letter half done,

"Tante Hildegard, to hear the end of it in heaven will be fun!"

A loving letter to Ruthie, full of praise to the Lord-

Telling of friends, Sisters Pickle and Flinn, having gone on before.

And dear brother Sam, our Mother's firstborn son,

So glad for your summer visit with Mother, tho' painfully done.

And loving Marvin, the youngest, you had a long talk on the phone

Just two days before Mother went home.

Dear Violet, loved by us all, especially by Mother,

Whom often you'd write, visit or call;

And faithful Esther and Wayne, daily burdens you did bear-

God will reward your constant, tender loving care!

So why are we sorrowing? Why are we sad?

Let us rather rejoice, be thankful and glad!

For the hope of reunion and love that endures,

Mother is safe in heaven, and in God's love, we're secure.

It seems when death strikes, one has a tendency to eulogize, and perhaps even exaggerate, the good qualities of the deceased and by the same token, blame oneself for neglects or misunderstandings. Although we five children all dearly loved Mother and knew likewise she loved us very much, yet we had to honestly admit that misunderstandings had developed—especially through the medium of letters during the latter months of Mother's life. We thought at times that perhaps she was just over-ripe for heaven. Rather than carry any burden of guilt, I encouraged each of us just to release all the memories to our heavenly Father, and he would save the wheat and burn the chaff. We know our love for each other is eternal.

For about a week after Mother's homegoing, I experienced an intermittent ache deep within my spirit. When the tape arrived in the mail on which Esther had recorded the memorial service, I was almost reluctant to listen to it for fear this would cut the wound of separation even more deeply. But I turned it on and was blessed to hear Mother's favorite hymns sung by the congregation and beautiful solos by Lorraine Sinner, and then Pastor Sinner's kind remarks and message, and also the loving tributes from Violet, Esther and Marvin.

Somehow when the recording of the service was ended, I just left the tape recorder on—while I sat there misty eyed. Suddenly, I was startled to hear a conversation between Esther and Mother that had been recorded two years previously on this same tape. As Esther was giving Mother a glowing report of a great church convention she had attended (together with me), Mother responded with delighted, joyous laughter. I could hardly believe my ears—the beginning of the tape bore Mother's memorial service and now at the end of the tape is Mother's voice with joyful laughter! In that very instant of almost disbelief, I had another peek into eternity where "God will wipe away all tears from their eyes, and there shall be no more death, nor sorrow, nor crying, nor pain. All of that has gone forever" (Revelations 21:4). Mother was truly laughing joyfully in the presence of her Lord.

My sorrow was turned into joy at that dramatic moment, and for days afterwards I felt Mother very close to me. As I envisioned her, she seemed to be looking down from the edge of eternity with a radiant smile on her face, with the lightheartedness of a young child skipping along in a field of flowers.

God Recycles **Broken** *Dreams*

The peace and joy of her new state of release permeated my own spirit and my sorrow was turned into joy.

So even though we must walk through the valleys of suffering, and at times through the shadow of death, how blessed it is to catch glimpses at the edge of eternity and be assured it is all there as he has promised. What a blessed hope we have!

Chapter 9
Child of Promise

When God desired to reveal himself to the human family, he chose the form of a helpless babe. When Jesus sought to illustrate the Kingdom of God, he beckoned to a little child and placed him in the midst of his followers. It is an awesome experience to have a child placed in the midst of our hearts and homes... or neighborhood, or church, for "every child is a new thought of God." Somehow his unspoiled humility and unpretentious honesty exposes the deceitful pride and protective dishonesty of the adult façade. Mystically, a young child seems to accept God without the need to hide his humanity.

It was for ten long years that we had longed and prayed for such a little life to bless our home. We had suffered the disappointing loss of a full-term stillborn infant son during the second year of our marriage. What a painful experience that was to have to bury our expectant dreams and the accumulated anticipations of nine months of attachment. Then to have to return home from the hospital with empty hands and aching hearts was unspeakably traumatic. Tearfully, I packed away all the little garments, blankets, bibs, and baby toys that had been so lovingly given at two baby showers. As I was tucking them away, I wondered how long it would be before I would be taking them out again.

What I had thought might be an interval of just one or two years stretched out to ten long years filled with all the frustrations of unfulfilled longings, medical tests and treatments—and just waiting. I could empathize with Hannah who "… was in deep anguish and was crying bitterly as she prayed to the Lord" for a son (I Samuel 1:10). There were so many painful reminders that my husband and I were childless—every time we would receive a birth announcement from other young couple friends, I would rejoice with them, but at the same time wonder, *will our turn ever come?*

Even when we would drive by yards where diapers were blowing in the breeze on the clotheslines (dryers were scarce in those days), I would find myself almost envious of that obvious symbol of motherhood. Then there were those dreadful Mother's Day observances in various churches of which we were a part where each mother in attendance would be presented a small potted plant or another special token of honor; I almost wished I could absent myself on such occasions. In retrospect, if only those in charge could have recognized the fact that every normal woman is potentially a mother at heart, and in fact, often "mothers" more children than those who have children by birth.

Indeed, we did "parent" many children in the communities in which we lived during those ten years of childlessness. Somehow the word got around that the Shanks usually had a cookie jar full of homemade goodies, a box of used toys and games… and most of all, listening ears and hearts of love for those little ones who needed more attention than their tired parents seemed able to give. Especially at Easter and Christmas it was a gratifying experience to be able to select holiday gifts and candies for the needy children in our area.

As friends and relatives observed our intense love for children, they would frequently suggest, "Why don't you adopt a child?"

Although I deeply admire those who have chosen this responsibility of love, I, personally, had felt restrained from taking this direction. In fact, I knew a child would be born to us for about three years in advance. This assurance came to me one day while reading Psalm 113 KJV: when I reached verse nine,

God Recycles Broken Dreams

the words seemed to enlarge in illuminated boldness: "He maketh the barren woman to keep house, and to be a joyful mother of children. Praise ye the Lord." From that moment on, I envisioned a little cherub named Beverly Sue floating around on a cloud up there somewhere. After that, when someone would suggest our adopting a baby, my reply would be, "The Lord is getting Beverly Sue ready for us!"

As is so often true, dreams are fulfilled in most unexpected and even at times, in traumatic ways. As a result of an impossible situation for me—endeavoring to teach a class of 18 emotionally disturbed children—I was physically depleted. In the course of a medical check-up, the doctor diagnosed a severe iron deficiency in my blood and prescribed two iron shots per week. How remarkable that God can convert the bad in our lives for our good, for it was through this very difficult teaching assignment, almost shattering my ego because of my inadequacy, that I was brought physically low enough to seek and find the very help my body was needing to conceive and carry Beverly Sue. Truly, "… All things work together for good…" as we love and trust God (Romans 8:28).

Although my dream had envisioned Beverly Sue floating along very peacefully on a billowy cloud, she started her voyage to earth on a rocky road instead. I was "seasick" unceasingly for the first several months until I actually started to wonder why I had ever even wanted a baby! That tumultuous beginning was aggravated by a seven-thousand-mile round trip by car from Pennsylvania to California. This was a planned joint celebration of our tenth wedding anniversary together with my husband's completion of his second college degree. But this had been planned before we were aware that Beverly was a stowaway passenger on this trip. What an unforgettable trip that was—with my increasing nausea, the trash cans along the highways became our most looked-for tourist attraction! By the time we had returned home to our parishioners in Pennsylvania, they hardly recognized me because I had lost over twenty pounds in less than a month.

But, again, new life came forth out of seemingly near death. As the distress subsided, my joys of expectation were unquenchable. How proudly I wore my maternity outfits! During the long winter evenings my hands were busy at work embroidering infant's garments. In the daytime, I spent happy hours decorating the little nursery, and with a final touch hung up pictures of the four famous Northern Tissue winsome girls. Borrowing a sewing machine, I sewed yards of light lavender taffeta skirting with nylon ruffles and bows around a bassinet. When friends would ask quite honestly, "But what if it's a boy?" I would calmly reassure them (and myself!), "Oh, but we've been expecting Beverly Sue for three years already!"

True to style, Beverly arrived through intense struggle and anguish, but much to our joy she was alive and well! I recall while in delivery hearing the kind voice of Dr. Cunningham urging the attending nurses, "These folks had a stillborn ten years ago and have desperately wanted another baby ever since—let's do all we can!"

Truly they did—even though Beverly kept them awake at 2:45 in the morning with some complications. By nine o'clock that morning, the exciting news of her arrival had flashed through our friendly neighborhood and community, and what a joy it was to receive over one hundred congratulatory cards, as well as many gifts from friends, far and near, who had been rooting for us all those years! It seemed like Christmas in March.

Yet in the midst of all these joys, again there were stressful moments—the frustrations of establishing a satisfactory formula, the loss of sleep while trying to obtain relief for the baby's tummy cramps and all the other uncertainties of caring for our baby. At times all these new dilemmas drew my husband and me together as we sought solutions; but in other instances, we found ourselves so independently concerned for our precious cherub that we would suddenly find ourselves in tense opposition. We discovered this new bundle would force a new growth within ourselves and our relationship.

God Recycles **Broken** *Dreams*

There were times when I felt these new responsibilities were greater than what I had anticipated, but I learned that the rewards of motherhood far outweighed the self-sacrifice required.

To celebrate that first real Mother's Day for me, Beverly sent the following note of thanks to Dr. Cunningham (with a little assistance, of course!):

> Dear Dr. Cunningham,
>
> This is my first attempt at writing a letter (since I'm only seven weeks old), so I may say things a little awkwardly, but I felt I had a few things to say to you. First, I want to tell you how very happy my Mommy and Daddy are to have me; often they gaze upon me admiringly and tell me that I am the perfect fulfillment of their dreams and prayers of ten years. They seem to think I'm so special that they even call me their "little cherub." Since I have received such a very warm welcome not only by my parents, but also by their friends, I feel I want to thank you for all you did in helping me to have a safe arrival. I know you helped to make Mommy strong so she could "carry" me and then when I was pushing my way into the world, I could hear your kind and patient words. I shall always be grateful and just hope I can spread as much sunshine and happiness in my little way as you have in your big way.
>
> Happy-to-be-alive,
>
> Beverly Sue Shank

For her first birthday, I was inspired to write this poem which accompanied her picture in the local newspaper:

The Greatest Wonder

We gaze upon a handsome spire
Made by man and with awe admire;

The house, the bridge and highway, too
Demand great skill by not a few.

But the greatest beauties we can find
Are products of a higher mind;
Surely the rainbow, trees, and flowers,
Birds and beasts bespeak this Power.

But the crowning glory of his creation,
Loved by folk of every nation,
Is a babe—so wondrous fair,
Far beyond any earthly compare.

He reflected the twinkle of starry skies
Deep into bright and sparkling eyes;
And molded pink hued petals of the rose
Into chubby cheeks and cute little toes.

He captured the radiance and warmth of the sun
To span many smiles in response to some fun;
And transformed the brook's refreshing gurgles
Into delightful coos and spontaneous giggles.

Yes, take all the beauties of earth combined,
None more perfect will you find
Than a babe—a priceless treasure,
Ours to love without measure!

Even after having moved from that community, we kept in touch with this very special doctor until we sadly learned of his death. In response to Beverly's second birthday letter and picture, Dr. Cunningham took time out of a busy

God Recycles **Broken** *Dreams*

seminar in Madrid, Spain (actually, probably less busy than his strenuous "on call" availability while serving his community) to pen the following reply:

> My dear Beverly Sue:
>
> It was so nice of you to write me such a good letter telling me all about yourself on your second birthday. You are rapidly becoming quite a young lady and it makes me happy to know that you are giving mother and dad so much happiness. Please keep in touch with me—I'll always be glad to hear from you. Mrs. Cunningham and I are spending a short two weeks in Madrid while I am doing some work at the university. This is a beautiful city and Spain is all that history has recorded. Thanks very much for writing to me.
>
> Sincerely yours,
>
> Dr. Cunningham

Realizing that what a child learns during the first five formative years of his life is more than the sum total of the remainder of his life puts an awesome responsibility upon the shoulders of parents. I am sympathetically aware that there are varying circumstances making it necessary for baby-sitters to care for our children, but we very jealously arranged to spend optimum hours with our very eager-to-learn child. This would involve excursions to the library and bringing home armloads of books; already at age two we made the bedtime story a priority. We made many trips to the park to visit the swings and slides, and had fun times at the beach. It seemed like Beverly's ears and eyes were ever open and alert to see and hear new sights and sounds in her ever-widening world—what an irreplaceable reward of parenthood to be a part of this growing miracle!

Concerned that Beverly should not live up to the carelessly placed stigma of "a spoiled, only child," we welcomed neighborhood children in our yard and home until we would almost have to set up a restraining schedule. At a very young age, Beverly was an aggressive leader of her playmates, but this quality had to be tempered. How humiliating to me to have a neighbor mother ring our doorbell and show me Beverly's teeth marks on her tearful daughter's arm; an apology and proper discipline terminated that form of misbehavior.

All of this interaction allowed for growth and direction; even children, when given rights and restrictions, learn to know themselves while playing with others. Of course, sometimes needless self-doubts arise during this interaction. For example, one time some of Beverly's older playmates scared her by saying she would have to go to speech class once she started school because she just could not handle all the sounds yet. One night while taking her bath, with deep concern she asked me, "Mommy, when I go to school, will I have to go to 'peech' class?" (Those sp's just had not developed yet!)

For Beverly's third birthday, this poem expressed my feelings about her:

Our Angel

Three years ago today
A little cherub flew our way
From heavenly abode up above
Into our waiting home of love.

Of course she's dearer every day,
Even though quite oft she wants her way;
But that is part of growing up—
The wants and wishes to develop.

She has her share of spunk and wit
And lacks for charm not a bit.
The longer the legs, the shorter the wings,
But oh, the joy that she brings!

God Recycles **Broken** *Dreams*

If out of a million we'd have our choice

Of blonde or brunette girls and boys,

Without hesitation she'd rate 1st pick,

For she's our angel—altho' not angelic!

Not only was it helpful for Beverly's development to have interaction with other growing children, but I found it extremely helpful for me, as a growing mother, to watch other children and their parents in action. From some I gained a necessary balance—like the time I had Beverly all dressed up to attend her twin friends' birthday party. As the children were having a romping good time in the yard, the father of Randy and Andy observed my over-protective care of my little "Miss Prissy," he pulled me into tow, "Ruth, why don't you let Beverly enjoy herself—a little water will wash away all the dirt!"

Then there were scenes which infuriated me—parents screaming at their little defenseless children, impatient mothers slapping the hands of these little curious ones while shopping, proud parents competing with others in the neighborhood to see who could toilet train their child first—irrespective of individual rates of development. The outcome of all this was the following poem which I had printed and distributed freely:

Please Understand Me

Please be careful with my feelings

They're the only ones I've got.

If you just try to understand me,

I will learn and grow a lot.

Please don't embarrass me

In front of all the others;

What little faith I have in me

This all somehow smothers.

My feelings are like a see-saw
Sometimes they're up, sometimes they're down;
But they balance so much better
When you give me smiles instead of frowns.

Sometimes I get a bright idea,
And am proud to tell you so;
But if you mock and don't receive it,
My feelings get a terrible blow.

Just like a flower unfolding
And a tree growing high,
I want to unfold and grow up;
Don't tramp on me when I try.

So, be careful with my feelings,
For they are really me;
And "me" is the only one I'll ever know
And the only one I'll ever be!

As part of the growing up process, there were those frightening moments—like the morning Beverly was sitting in her highchair enjoying her Cheerios, which usually involved her new skill of counting them, when suddenly I noticed she had discovered a new place for her Cheerios other than her mouth; she thought she would try stuffing them into her nostrils. My husband initiated a quick rescue operation by sprinkling ground pepper on his hand and holding it beneath Beverly's nose. It worked within seconds, and Cheerios were being sneezed out all over the place!

An even more frightening experience took place during kindergarten. One day after her class, she was to eat lunch and spend the afternoon with friends.

God Recycles **Broken** *Dreams*

It was during their lunch time that I happened to be in a music store about fifteen miles from there, when suddenly I sensed a heavy, almost choking cloud of sorrow settle upon my spirit. It was so intense that I left the store and hurried to my car. As I glanced through the Bible and lifted my thoughts toward God, a love for Beverly overwhelmed me—it was as if my whole inner being was reaching out to her in love. With that the heavy cloud lifted. I resumed my activities and almost forgot the whole thing until I stopped to get Beverly, at which time the mother of that household met me with, "Did we ever have a scare with Beverly today!"

"What happened?" I inquired anxiously.

"Well, she and my children were sitting at the table eating lunch when the doorbell rang. While I went to answer the door, one of my boys offered Beverly a large gumball."

I could almost guess the rest, for I had never given her any of these large gumballs. "Did she have trouble with it?" I pursued.

"She sure did… evidently after partially chewing it, it got stuck in her throat, and she could not seem to get it up or swallow it down."

"Oh, God," I interjected, "that must have been just the time I felt that tremendous love for her and reached out simultaneously to God and her— how faithful and good God is!"

"I was really frightened," the friend continued, "For a minute or so I just didn't know what to do, but all of a sudden the gumball loosened and Beverly was able to cough it up."

How God does care for these little ones!

There were also the fun times and memories of birthday parties at the park or petting zoo. With Beverly's birthday coming shortly before Easter, I can recall having prepared sandwiches cut in bunny and chick designs, a big bunny cake, sprinkled with coconut and jelly bean eyes and pipe cleaner whiskers.

And of course, pin-the-tail (cotton) on the rabbit and an Easter egg hunt as some of the games. At the end of one of those happy occasions, Beverly prayed in her little childish way, "Thank you, Jesus, for letting everybody love me."

Also, there were the extended trips from Florida to New York and from Florida to California. For each of these we would "borrow" someone's child as a travel pal for Beverly—a duo blessing—to give this child an opportunity she otherwise would not have had and to give Beverly company. Over the long miles we would improvise all kinds of travel games—finding the ABC's in progressive sequence from highway signs, counting brown cows versus black ones, compiling lists of states from license plates, making up stories and poems with each member contributing parts. And of course, as Mom would cook a camp meal, Dad would romp and climb trees with the youngsters. Sure, there were times of stress and fatigued nerves, but the non-quenchable flame of love for God and each other would warm our hearts again. Truly, "Most important of all, continue to show deep love for each other, for love makes up for many of your faults" (I Peter 4:8).

This love takes new directions and expression as we grow along with our children in their adolescent and teenage years. Although as concerned parents we must always be alert and available to the needs of children, yet there must be a gradual loosening of the reins to allow their independence and responsibility to develop. For example, being quite school-oriented, I would often find myself pressing Beverly into getting her homework assignments. But when I backed off and transferred that responsibility upon her shoulders, there was much less stress between us and her work was done—most of the time. So often the pride of parents is so tightly interwoven with our requirements of our children that they are not allowed to experience the consequences of their own choices. Our love releases them to find their own identity.

Also we must be aware of our children's potential and interests and as much as possible, provide instruction in these areas. It often required sacrifice of both

God Recycles **Broken** *Dreams*

time and finance to allow Beverly to take ballet, baton twirling, trumpet, organ, horseback riding, and although she has not become a professional performer in any of these areas, yet I feel her exposure to them has been a worthwhile investment. Our love will be sacrificial but without excessive expectation.

To respect our children's choices and wishes is increasingly important as their world expands. Again, we should set up perimeters of guidance and of values, but within those limitations, they should be allowed personal choices. This has been my policy with Beverly in shopping for her clothing—even from a very young age; she could choose colors, styles, and materials as long as the items selected were within a suggested price range. Our love respects their choices.

Should our child choose values contrary to ours in their older years, I feel we must still communicate our love and acceptance of them. Speaking the truth in love is important, but so is letting them know we will never reject them if their behavior is contrary to our standards. Love accepts our children even if we must reject their behavior.

There have been numerous times in Beverly's process of maturing—in seeking to establish her own identity that she and I have had some "up-tight," almost explosive, encounters. In those times, I would remind her that no matter what was "bugging" either one of us, we must talk it over. If I over-reacted during such times, I felt it necessary to take the lead in apologizing. Children respect the honest parent. This respect cannot be demanded… it must be earned. Our love for our young folk must be honest and humble.

Probably some of our most meaningful times together have been those unplanned times when Beverly would just flop over my bed and start sharing the accumulated thoughts and stresses of her world. Being of a very sensitive, perceptive nature, she has suffered much stress with the insensitivity and low value system of her peers. Having absented herself from a youth group because of the unproductive time spent there, she received a phone call from one of the appointed members for this task. "That same girl never even looks at me when I do attend," Beverly observed. "How can she be so 'friendly' and miss me all of a sudden? That group is so boring I wouldn't invite my worst enemy to go with me!"

Observing the fad of high school kids wearing T-shirts conveying sacreligious messages such as, "Love thy neighbor, but don't get caught," Beverly reflected, "Why when they say they don't believe in God, why do they skirt all around him? If God is nothing then they should say nothing about nothing."

In commenting on a P. E. teacher who had treated some pupils most inhumanely, Beverly said, "I pity Mrs. __. She's so unstable and her ego is threatened so quickly."

When I called the principal about that particular incident, he hedged and dodged the issue. Beverly summed it up with, "Now—that's a worldly man!"

Sometimes these sharing times would extend into a late hour, at which time I would remind Beverly gently, "You need to get to bed, Beverly, so you can handle tomorrow."

Her quick retort would be, "If I'm awake I can't handle it!" Our love for our growing youth… listens!

This listening has not been one-sided. Often in the pressures of life with its complexities, I needed that listening ear. Being extremely exhausted and overworked at my job, I complained, "This is no way to live," to which Beverly responded in her own inimical way, "But a sure way to die!"

"Beverly, you're too smart," I replied, and again with gunfire rapidity she shot back with, "You're too dumb!" (To work that hard).

Really true! Another time when I had experienced a spiritual battle all day previously to starting a Parent's Class, Beverly observed, "Of course, the devil wouldn't help you launch this class—unless it would be a rocket with a self-destructive gadget inside of it."

God Recycles **Broken** *Dreams*

Complimenting me on my message to a church, she said, "Mom, you keep it moving, interesting, clear thinking, and everything you say counts—it's pure cream!"

Speaking of cream, on one occasion when we were discussing the seeming shortage of available nice guys for dates, I tried to encourage Beverly by saying, "Cream always comes to the top... keep your ideals high and you'll meet someone who will respect them;" to which she retorted, "Where do you find cream when all the cows are sick?"

But Beverly's sensitive nature does not operate just in the detection of the false and negative; she often expresses this beautiful asset in positive ways. Noticing that her high school counselor appeared very weary, Beverly said, "I must get a rose to take to Mrs.____; she looks so worn!"

It was months later that I learned from this counselor that during that period when Beverly had given her a lovely rose, the counselor was going through a traumatic divorce, and how that rose spoke volumes of love and hope of new life.

Also, Beverly is one of the most meticulous, precise shoppers for gifts I've had the joy of knowing. I will never forget the appropriate items she chose to stuff my very first Christmas stocking—bath oil in grape cluster containers, (I love grapes!), Baby Ruth candy bars, a paddle with a ball on an elastic band (a favorite toy from childhood) and a cute bean-bag orange kitty (symbolic of my wish for a live orange cat). Often Beverly presented me with very lovely pieces of her handcraft and art—delicately assembled from sprigs of flowers, driftwood, leather, a little deer mounted on a plaque, or a lovely Cypress Gardens decoupage.

Speaking of decoupage, after Beverly had volunteered many hours of library work for the historical society of a town where we lived, an honorary member who was nearly blind presented Beverly with a delightful book of poems she had authored. Catching the theme of this book, Of A Number *of Things*, Beverly found R. L. Stevenson's quote, "This world is so full of a number of things, I'm sure we should all be as happy as kings," on a cute card, decoupaged it on a plaque, and mailed it to this fine elderly lady. Thoughtfulness of others—especially of the elderly—is high on the totem pole of my evaluation of a person.

While a junior in high school, Beverly had an English assignment to write a letter to an imaginary friend telling about the generation gap in her family. This was her letter in part:

> "I do not think there is a generation gap in my family. I do not wish to bore you with complaints that we get along fine, but it seems necessary that I should do so.
>
> I must tell you why there is not a generation gap in our family. There was never a need for one. I know it sounds silly, but we get along fine without it. We ignore it and it ignored us. Our fights (disagreements) were very lively by themselves and with no need for outside assistance.
>
> Secondly, my mother and I agree on every major issue that might arise. I apologize for that, for I'm sure it deprives this letter of any excitement it might have had. However, we do have a lot of "discussions" on minor issues such as cleaning my room or other silly things—but they're fun."

The teacher's red ink comment in the margin read, "Thank goodness, some families escape the torment inherent in an acute generation gap!"

Yes, thank God, for the possibility and provisions of living our lives before our children so that when all is said and done, they know we love them.

God Recycles **Broken** *Dreams*

Chapter 10
The Miracle House

After six months of being grateful recipients of the gracious hospitality of my sister and brother-in-law, I felt I had regained sufficient physical and emotional stability to set up housekeeping again. I contacted several realtors within the East Bay area of San Francisco, and I was house-hopping for the next several weeks. A realtor would call and say "Ruth, I have just what you're looking for… can I pick you up at 10:30 this morning to show you this winner?"

I would comply, but repeatedly be distressed to find these 'just what you're looking for' houses to be exactly the opposite!—something I would never have envisioned in a nightmare. So after several weeks of fruitless frustrations, I cried to the Lord in desperation, "Please, Lord, *you* lead me to the home you know will be just right for us."

Before that day had pulled its shades for the night, my searching was over. I had a divine Realtor who really knew what I was looking for!

But, of course, as is usually the case, God gave me directions through a normal procedure. My sister, Esther, had suggested, "Ruthie, there's an ad in today's paper that sounds rather good. Let's drive over to Pinole and check it out."

Pinole was a quiet, homey town with a population of about 15,000 nestled among the rolling hills, with its cattle and horses grazing leisurely and within easy reach of the freeway and shopping centers. Although the advertised house was a disaster, God used that visit to lead us on an extended search within this appealing community. "Let's just drive around in Pinole since we're already here," I suggested to Esther, "and just check any 'For Sale' properties."

To ask admission to see a house without a realtor was contrary to usual decorum, I realized, but somehow I sensed the invisible presence of my divine Realtor by my side. In my search that day, I almost passed up "the winner" just because of an unsightly juniper bush that betrayed the hidden beauty of this cozy home, and isn't this rather typical of how we often allow one undesirable feature to deprive us of many beautiful experiences in life!

As soon as the door was opened by a gracious lady and my eyes caught a glimpse of the cozy, homey interior, I knew in an instant that this was to be our home! Before I had even completed the tour through this lovely home, my heart was turning flip-flops of joy and praise to God for having led us so beautifully. Then as we stepped outside to the backyard, I was almost ecstatic with joy to behold a miniature paradise—with the ivy-covered banks, a wide expanse of lawn outlined by a beautiful assortment of trees and shrubbery, and a kidney-shaped garden in which I could envision a lovely fountain (which later was placed there). The lovely fruitless mulberry (thank God it was fruitless!) even had a circular wooden bench around its base. Someone had really cared about this place and now I would be the benefactor.

Within thirty minutes of having returned back to Esther's home, I received a call from Trudy, the realtor I had favored during my previous weeks of searching. "I have three places I'd like to show you, Ruth," she said.

"I feel I've already located the one I want," I informed her, "but I'm willing to check them out."

The first two houses Trudy took me to were nice, but not for me. Was I ever excited when the third one she drove to was the very one I had been led to earlier that afternoon! "Trudy, that's the one I saw about an hour ago, and I just fell in love with it!"

God Recycles **Broken** *Dreams*

"Well then, why don't you just wait here in the car while I go in to check it out?"

When Trudy returned to the car she, too, was effervescent. "Oh, Ruth, I can see that is exactly what you have been looking for. It just somehow looks like you!"

Then she went on to explain, "I've had this house in my listings for several weeks, but I didn't offer to show it to you before today because it was really out of your price range. Just today the price came down $3,000!"

"Oh, Father, you are so good! And always right on time!"

Now that God had helped me locate this adorable home, I would need a miracle to finance it—especially since I had not even secured a job yet. Scraping together a meager savings of previous years, together with a loan, I took care of the necessary down payment. My kind brother-in-law let me make the bank loan in his name because of my lack of equity. From then on the monthly mortgage payments were often challenges, but always the need was met—a miracle of God's love, indeed.

Within weeks, Beverly and I were happy residents in this attractive area, which was situated on a hill overlooking the sprawling high school that Beverly would attend. Although our home was still sparsely furnished, I felt impelled to go from room to room just praising God for this wonderful haven of rest. I reminded him that it was his and our home together—asking his blessing within every room and for his benediction to rest upon everyone who would enter this abode. Invariably, as visitors came, they sensed the presence of God's love.

Having brought just a few basic pieces of furniture along in our move from New Jersey to California earlier that year, we now needed guidance in finding furniture bargains. What a rewarding adventure with God that was!

One Saturday evening I prayed, "Lord, I really need a pole light by my organ, and since our home is in colonial colors, please help me locate a handsome colonial pole light at a reasonable price."

The very next day, I spotted an ad in the newspaper, "Maple hutch, pole light, like new, reasonable." Locating the address in a community about twenty miles east of us, I was delighted to find a beautiful maple pole light with three torch-like lamps. The lady of the house was in the process of changing her décor from early American to Mediterranean, and as a result I became the happy benefactor of the $85 light for just $15, and a charming maple hutch for about 1/3 of its original selling price. Noticing two lovely maple step-end tables with louvered doors and a matching coffee table, I inquired, "Do you plan to sell these also?"

"I'll need to give that more thought, but why don't you call me back later in the week, and I can tell you what I've decided to do concerning them."

That just gave me more time to talk to my Father about them. By Friday of that week, the Lord had arranged it all—the owner had decided to sell the tables at a "give-away" price. As a bonus, she and her husband offered to personally deliver all these beautiful maple items in the husband's company truck. "Oh, God, you are so good!"

One Sunday morning before heading off to Sunday school, I mentioned to my sister who had stopped by, "Right over in that area of the living room is where I'd like a small maple Magnavox stereo." (I've learned that God rather likes our specific requests; it seems to delight his heart to realize he makes possible the just-what-I-wanted item!)

When I envisioned this stereo, I'd felt possibly within the next few months it might be a reality, but in his usual style, our God does "… exceeding, abundantly above all that we can ask or think" and by evening of that same day we had lovely stereo music filling our home. Let me tell you how that came about.

God Recycles Broken Dreams

Just as I was approaching the church where I taught Sunday school, I noticed a garage sale sign. Bev, also noticing the sign, verbalized what I was thinking. "Mom, there's a garage sale… they might have some things we're needing."

Glancing at my watch and with a losing argument that we did not have the time to spare, I found myself turning into the driveway of that home. As we quickly walked into the garage cluttered with all kinds of household items, I almost thought I was dreaming to behold a small maple Magnavox stereo with two external speakers! Approaching the owner, I hastily explained, "I'm very much interested in your stereo here, but I've got an appointment with a Sunday school class in about seven minutes, so I'll be back later. I wish you could save it for me."

Sensing his reluctance, I knew just what to do next to put a "hold" on it. Arriving at my junior high class, almost breathless, I challenged them to join me in prayer for God to keep a reserve on that stereo at the garage sale just a few blocks from our class. Now that was putting God "on the spot" for those eager junior highers, and you don't think God would let them down, do you?

Hurrying back to the garage sale ("You'll have to forgive me this time, pastor, for skipping church"), I noticed people dangerously close to "my stereo." Hastening over to the owner, I asked if I might have a demonstration of the stereo, and after a few moments, the transaction was made… a $240 item sold for just $85. In the meantime, Bev had spotted a push lawnmower outside the back exit for just $2.50. That mower served us well for 5 years. (I well recall my sense of satisfaction when my neighbor asked to borrow my old reliable pusher when her much more expensive power mower failed).

God does not always give us everything we ask for immediately; actually, such treatment could spoil us—besides preventing the flexing of our faith muscles. For about two years, I tolerated an inadequate, fading green sofa in our living room, but desired a more suitable colonial sofa. One day while checking out an advertised used TV for my mother, I learned that an almost new colonial sofa was also for sale at the same residence. When I beheld that beautiful luxurious sofa, I questioned the lady of the house, "Why are you selling this sofa?"

"Oh, I had it custom-made and when it was delivered I realized it was really too large for my room; so now, I want to sell it and quickly buy another one before my husband retires." (Bless that husband, Lord!)

I learned it had been purchased at the most elite furniture store in the area and had reversible cushions with maximum support coils. She quoted a selling price of just $150 (originally it was about $600). Taking measurements of it, I told her I would call her back the next day on my decision. When I did call her, she volunteered, "My husband said to let you have it for $130."

"Wow, Lord, that's even less than half price... actually less than one fourth its original price. We're getting better deals all the time! Thanks so much!"

Then I had the problem of getting that large sofa transported across town to my home. Soon the Lord reminded me that he just never does things halfway—if he starts a project, he will complete it. In the course of our telephone conversation, the owner of the sofa learned that I was a neighbor to one of her best friends and suggested this neighbor's husband would be glad to pick up the sofa in his truck, which he did. Refusing my offer of reimbursement, he did get a home-made strawberry pie which seemed to suit his taste just fine.

So it was piece by piece, in beautiful, miraculous ways and means, that our home was furnished. Let me share God's guidance in selecting a washing machine. Becoming somewhat weary of having to drag our laundry down to the public laundromat, I prayed one day, "Lord, I would like so much to have our own washer. You know how our garage has a wash sink with plumbing all ready for a washer. I won't bother you for a dryer, for you're quite generous with year-round breezes in this area. But now, Lord, my funds are rather limited, so please help me to get a good used washing machine for $35."

 God Recycles **Broken** *Dreams*

I realized that was restricting the Lord to a tight budget, but as usual, he came through all right. Within that week, there were two ads in the newspaper for used washers, and each listed for $35. Calling both phone numbers, I sensed which one I should pursue and was very pleased with the one that was delivered for that price by a young husband and father. He was attending classes in appliance repairs, selling washers for a side income.

Upon delivery and during the "test run" of the used washer, I sensed a deep spiritual need within this young man, and prayed for him frequently after that. It was just about three months later that I was joyfully surprised to see him in attendance at a religious gathering. "What in the world are you doing here, Gary?" I inquired.

To which he replied with a radiant smile, "Oh, both my buddy and I gave our lives over to Jesus Christ recently; we've been delivered from alcohol."

It seemed that whenever my washer was in need of added attention, Gary was in need of spiritual strengthening; so we just exchanged skills. I surely received maximum benefits from such a minimal investment.

This was how the Lord blessed and guided us in furnishing every room. Whenever some repair or renovation project was needed, I would seek his guidance. It was almost amusing at times how, with my lack of skills, by thumping on a pipe or by loosening or tightening a screw, drips in pipes would cease and clocks would start ticking again. It was almost as if God's strength and wisdom were made perfect in my weakness.

Just as God blessed our home, so Satan, our ever-present enemy lurking about to "… steal, kill and destroy…" (John 10:10), made several attempts to harm our property. High school students "on the loose" during off-periods roamed the community and just for "kicks" perpetuated a rash of break-ins. Our lovely home was a victim of such vagrancy twice with every room ransacked. Not finding many valuables other than Bev's babysitting savings and our tape recorder, probably as a last stroke of contempt they grabbed cereal out of the kitchen cupboard and tossed it all over the rug. Also, they had ripped off the beautiful mother-of-pearl covers from a New Testament, a gift from Jerusalem. Such brazen behavior!

Not only did our heavenly Father direct our steps in securing our home, then in furnishing it, but also he was very much in charge of our selling it. Even before it was clear that God had another assignment for me, which would necessitate a move across the country, I experienced a gradual weaning from this home that I had come to love.

When I knew for certain I would be moving, I had an appointment with the Lord during which time I prayed, "Father, you have so wonderfully provided for us during these past five years in allowing us to have this adorable home. Now I release it all back to you and ask you to bless the right people with this house and furniture."

It was by way of a casual remark during a phone conversation with a neighbor that a buyer was located—"I want you to know we're in the process of selling our home and I thought you might want to choose your new neighbors in case you know of anyone looking for a home in this area," I explained.

Within a few days, friends of these neighbors came to see our house and wanted to sign papers that same evening. The beneficial feature of the agreement (which proved God's continuing care for us) was that although we negotiated our business at the end of March, we could continue living in our home until mid-June when my job assignment would be completed.

As for the furniture, mostly by word of mouth it was sold within two or three days, and again because of unusual circumstances of the purchasers, most all of the pieces remained in our home until shortly before we had to leave the area. Just as each piece had been purchased with special guidance and joy, it seemed as if God directed buyers to come who were truly blessed by their purchase.

God Recycles **Broken** *Dreams*

Just one example of the joy of transferring ownership of possessions under divine direction was that involving our elegant maple dining room set—my special pride and joy. The Carnes family are very special friends in the family of God. Often Bob and Mary, the parents, had joined me at this table with others for Bible study and prayer. It was around this table that one of their daughters had received Jesus Christ as Savior. This dining room table was a veritable altar. Therefore, it was with tearful joy that the eldest daughter, Bobbie and her wonderful husband, John, became the owners of this beautiful set. After the last piece had been carried out and carefully placed in one of the three cars of the Carnes' caravan that night, we joined hands in the now empty dining room in a circle of prayer of thanksgiving. With misty eyes, Bobbie said to me tenderly, "Ruth, whenever we gather around your table, we'll send a prayer your way for God to bless you where you are."

What a painfully sweet way to part with one's possessions!

Chapter 11
Our Golden Chariot

"I'm sorry, Ma'am, your exhaust system is so badly rusted that I really can't guarantee the welding job I did on it."

That was the woeful report from the muffler shop repairman concerning our "Ole Faithful" '65 Buick Skylark. "In fact," he continued, "since I can't guarantee the welded spots to hold together even long enough to get you out of this garage, I'm not even going to charge you for my work. To fix it right would cost at least fifty dollars, and even then I'm not sure it would hold up."

"Well, Father, thanks for that favor, but what do I do now? You can see how my little car is becoming a jolly jalopy—the rubber has been stripped from one of the windows and with the rainy season fast approaching, I sure won't be able to keep dry. The upholstery has been splitting from deterioration and is literally falling apart! Lord, I'm going to need your help, and quite soon." True to the serviceman's prediction, before I had hardly pulled out of his garage, my little Buick sounded like an angry tractor; the holes had burst open again in the muffler system. It was quite embarrassing for me to drive home through my neighborhood in such a noisy fashion.

Day after day as I would walk from my school office to the parking lot, I would look upon my pitiful Skylark with its rusty freckles, and then I would look up and pray, "Father, this car really is a disgrace to both you and me. After all, you are the King of the Earth and that makes me a King's daughter

(Psalm 47:7). To drive a car that looks and sounds as bad as this one surely doesn't befit royalty!"

I have found that God delights in a challenge to meet the needs of his children. In fact, we are encouraged to "Put God to the test and see how kind he is" (Psalm 34:8). This does not always mean our needs will be met immediately; in this seeming delay we must exercise our trust and patience.

So it was on Columbus Day, a holiday from school, that I awakened Bev with, "Bev, want to go along to help look for another car?"

With such an invitation she almost jumped out of bed, for it was just the day before when I had complained about our hopeless heap that she had spoken words of faith, "Mom, probably tomorrow you'll get a new car!"

How could she miss out on this exciting adventure!

I also called my mother to pray for guidance to which she replied in God's authority, "You go, and God will help you, I know... I will pray."

Those were all words of encouragement, "But," I wondered, "Where do I begin to look?"

I never had had such a responsibility before, and with my limited mechanical knowledge, I was an easy prey for some slick salesman. Suddenly, I felt terribly alone and frightened, but as I lifted my spirit Godward, God's love overwhelmed my spirit reminding me that he had promised to be as a husband to me (Isaiah 54:5) and that I could count on him for wisdom and support. How quickly fears are transformed into faith in his presence!

My next inspiration was to call our school secretary whose husband had a position in a nearby Chrysler/Plymouth company. "Vivian," I inquired, "would you happen to know if Verl's company has any good used cars on the lot?"

"Oh, Ruth," she replied eagerly, "I just wish you could have seen the beauty Verl brought home last week; it was such a good deal that he wished he could somehow keep it in the family."

God Recycles **Broken** *Dreams*

"What make and color?" I pursued.

"Oh, a pretty amber bronze bottom with a beige hardtop but I don't know what make it is."

"That's the very color I've been admiring the most in recent months. What was the price tag on it?" I continued.

"I believe it was around $2,500."

"Well, that's out of my reach, but thanks anyway, Vivian."

Thinking more in terms of an older, cheaper model, Bev and I surveyed numerous car lots, especially favoring Buicks and Pontiacs since I had had previous positive experiences with those makes. But nothing seemed available that suited us.

Finally, almost as a last resort, I felt compelled to head for the Chrysler/ Plymouth show room. I informed Rick, the salesman, that we had come to see a used amber bronze with beige hardtop on his lot (quite a naïve introduction, I realize). Within moments we were standing beside this beautiful "golden chariot", and it was "love at first sight!" Listening to its commendable life story and all its fine features-- low mileage, one elderly owner, practically new steel radial tires and air-conditioning-- made me feel this was to be our car. Bev and I were transmitting silent messages to each other by our knowing glances—"This is it!"

When Rick commented further, "We rarely have a Buick on our lot, but this Skylark got here on a trade-in. There's nothing wrong with the car. The owner was retiring and wanted a new one."

I knew God had made special arrangements for us!

Then, inevitably came the realistic question, "What would be the down payment on this car?"

To which Rick replied, "Five hundred dollars."

I did not even have a fraction of that amount available, but I never winced, but rather continued, "And how much would the monthly payments be?"

"Approximately $120 a month," he answered matter-of-factly.

Maintaining the stance of a King's daughter (Psalm 45:9), but at the same time, aware that my budget could barely handle even one-third that amount, I responded as confidently as I dared, "Let me think about this overnight and then call you back in the morning."

"Fine," agreed Rick, "I'll put a 'hold' on it until tomorrow afternoon."

Hopping back into our worn, ten-year-old Skylark, Bev and I were almost ecstatic with joy. "Wow! That's our car. Praise God!"

Driving around the corner to Foster Freeze for a brief evening snack (with the help of a free coupon), I burst out with, "Father, I thank you for our (meaning his and our) car. I don't know just how we're going to pay for it, but that's your responsibility." Such audacity!

As we were enroute home, it suddenly dawned upon me that we had not even test-driven this car, quite contrary to usual procedure. But Bev quickly put me back on track with, "Mom, if you had, I would have felt it wasn't ours. Since it was ours, it wasn't even necessary to try it out!"

Stopping by the homes of Mother and my sister Esther, I announced that we had found our car. Mother said, "I knew that God would lead you to the right one."

Arriving home, I just flopped on the sofa, completely exhausted from the all-day search. Quieting my spirit, I sought audience with the Father again on this matter. "Lord, I'm not sure which direction you would like me to take. I begrudge paying high interest on a loan. Please let something better work out. I'm going to stand still and see the salvation of the Lord" (II Chronicles 20:17 KJV).

God Recycles **Broken** *Dreams*

During this resting time, the idea popped into my mind to call my ex-husband to see if he could possibly lend me the $500 for the down-payment, but instead, within minutes, he called, inquiring how everything was going for us. "Wow, Lord, what perfect timing!"

Sharing with him how we had looked at a good car deal, I inquired concerning his circumstances to which he responded, "Very fine. As a matter of fact, my sales of a particular item have far exceeded my greatest hopes."

It was a good time to approach him on the possibility of a loan for $500. He replied, "Give me a few moments to check up on some figures," and then he came back with this shocking announcement, "I really feel we ought to use our money rather than pay high interest. I feel I'd like to send you a check for $2,500."

I could hardly believe my ears. "But are you able to spare that much?" I queried in a trembling voice, "and how would you expect me to handle paying you back?"

"I realize you are operating on a very limited budget, so let's just not worry about it now; if sometime in the future I'm in need and you're in position to help me, we'll just handle it that way."

I was so overjoyed I could hardly sleep that night.

Eagerly the next morning I called Rick, the car salesman, "Rick, you can save that Skylark for me; I'll have a check for you by Friday."

"I already was told the good news by Verl," Rick replied, "looks like things really worked out for you. You don't have to wait until Friday to pick up the car. Stop by on Wednesday and I'll give you the keys."

After school on Wednesday, I stopped for Esther to go along to drive back my old car as I drove the new one. Rick, tilting back in his office chair, commented, "This is almost incredible, Ruth, how you're getting this car. I work twelve hours a day, six days a week, and things just don't happen like this!"

"I know, Rick, it does seem too good to be true, but when God is involved in a situation, nothing is impossible!"

As Rick proceeded to handle the paperwork, he questioned, "What do you plan to do with the old Skylark?"

"I thought I'd advertise it in the 'Family Fair' paper. Perhaps some young fellow would be interested in it."

"Are you aware that it has to be inspected before you can sell it?" he informed me.

"Oh, no, that would mean I'd have to spend at least fifty dollars for repairs on the exhaust system," I lamented.

Esther quickly came to the rescue with this proposal, "Why don't you just keep it, Rick, then I could ride home in her nice new air-conditioned one."

We did the paper work and found that the total cost was $2,988... $2,500 for the car and $488 in other fees and costs. After taking a look at my car, Rick offered me $188 for it, and with the $2,500 on its way I owed only $300 balance, for which Rick proceeded to make out loan payment papers. But by Friday not only had the check for $2,500 arrived in the mail, but also another check for the exact amount of $300. I laid both checks on my Bible and knelt in joyous and humble gratitude to such a wonderful God.

I could hardly wait to share this exciting news with Rick, but as I approached him in his office, he raised both hands in utter surrender and exclaimed, "My head has been spinning for two days from the last time you were here. I can't take anymore!"

As he escorted me to the clerk, instructing her to write out a receipt, "Paid in full," I interjected, "Rick, just let me show you the 'cherry on the sundae,'" and I proceeded to share with him how Bev had been admiring the Skylark key chains in a drugstore during previous months, and as we had gone the day before to get one, there were just a few car key chains thrown together on a summer closeout table. Among all that helter-skelter, was just one Skylark key chain and it was black suede with an amber bronze insignia, just the colors of our interior, and it had been reduced from $1.33 to $.68!

As Bev and I took our first ride in our beautiful "golden chariot" we invited Jesus to be our special passenger and requested an extra dispatch of angels to guard it. In fact, we decided our license tag bearing the letters DAP represented the insignia of Divine Agency Protection. My spirit soared with joyous gratitude, "I just love this car. It's not a thing. It's God in action!"

In retrospect, it is significant to me that our first weekend jaunt using our "new" car was a delightful trip along the rocky Pacific coast to Monterey and to Pacific Grove, the monarch butterfly capital of the world. Thousands of these gorgeous orange and black monarchs migrate to that particular area every fall, and to celebrate their arrival, the residents, including most of the schoolchildren, have a colorful parade with butterfly costumes and caterpillar floats. The colors of the monarch are almost the exact colors of our car—amber, black and beige. The whole concept of the release of the butterfly from a confined cocoon seemed to have its counterpart in the release within our own spirits. And the very title "Monarch" was a regal reminder that truly we are the King's daughters!

During the four years and 50,000 miles we drove the Skylark, we experienced repeatedly the protecting presence of our DAP. Probably the most outstanding example took place in Saskatchewan, Canada one summer when we traveled from California to Florida (via Canada)! Evidently becoming almost mesmerized by the seeming unending long stretch of road, Bev steered our car in the direction of a zooming car in the on-coming lane. Seeing the gravity of the situation, I snapped, "Bev, get in your lane!"

Her inexperience with power steering in such a critical situation resulted in over-steering, and within seconds, we were zigzagging across the highway like a drunken driver. Those frightening moments seemed like an eternity while I kept pleading, "Oh, Lord, help! Lord!"

Our escapade took us down an embankment, and with our rear wheels ripping over a cement culvert, we crunched to a grinding halt. Shaken and bruised, but still all in one piece, we stepped out of the car to view the damage—a scraped, dented fender, a sprung door, a deflated rear tire and a bent wheel. Within minutes a driver and his wife who had taken in the whole scene were at our side. "Are you ever (expletives deleted) lucky to be alive!" the man exclaimed.

Appreciating his support, I translated his oaths into, "We really praise God that we're alive!"

"About five different cars swerved out of your crazy path while you were out of control," he continued.

Truly it was God's mercies that spared us, as well as others, from death. "Many are the afflictions of the righteous; but the Lord delivers him out of them all. He keeps all his bones; not one of them is broken" (Psalm 34:19-20 KJV).

Being stranded on a very lonely stretch of road between Gull Lake and Swift Current and on Canada's national holiday (celebrating their 110th birthday), we were isolated down that embankment for about two hours before the necessary equipment came to our rescue. A Royal Canadian Mounted Police very kindly led us to the only body shop open in the area; the repairman took one look underneath our damaged car and stated, "My insurance man would consider this a 'total' because of the bent frame."

But after some straightening, we decided to proceed cautiously. That evening as we were unpacking our bags in a motel, I discovered a small Scripture card that had somehow gotten lost in the bottom of a bag; it bore this message: "But the mercy of the Lord is from everlasting to everlasting upon them that fear him and his righteousness unto children's children" (Psalm 103:17 KJV). And

God Recycles **Broken** *Dreams*

as I opened my Bible for my "good-night snack" my eyes scanned the verse I had just underlined that morning. "...those that listen shall live..." (John 5:25). I felt this had been an invaluable, although frightening, lesson for Bev in her early driving career, to be alert and receptive whenever controlling that much horsepower on the highway.

Not only was our Heavenly Father very much involved in the selection, payment and protection of our "golden chariot", but he also had been an integral part of its upkeep (after all, we are co-owners—God and I).

Another favor God arranged involving our car was in the matter of obtaining a set of steel radial tires. I had purchased such a set of nationally advertised tires before starting on our journey from California to Florida. After some months of residence in Florida, I became aware of a problem with one of the tires which caused increasing vibrations. Having it checked at a local tire company of that particular brand, I was told that the tire was breaking down inside. Since they did not carry the size I needed, they recommended I try the warehouse in the greater Orlando area. Unfortunately they did not have that size in stock either, so they offered to place an order for one at an out-of-state supply house.

After two weeks of increasing vibrations and with still no arrival of my ordered tire, I felt I should return to the local outlet again and ask for a special favor. I simply stated my case, "If I'm having this much difficulty in replacing this one tire, what happens when I'll need other replacements? Furthermore, when I bought this set of tires originally, I was told by the man who balanced them that they really were not in as good a "round" as they should have been, but since I was in the process of moving, I proceeded with them. Really, Sir," I continued, while breathing a silent prayer, "I feel I should think in terms of a full new set. What can you do to help me?"

He started flipping pages in the large manual studying the sizes and prices listed. He quoted the list price on my present tires and also a considerably higher price on an even better set. "I'm just not sure, lady," he said cautiously, "but I'll have to go measure how much of the tread you've worn; if it's more than one-third, I couldn't allow you any credit toward new ones."

While he stepped outside to make this measurement, I kept reminding the Father, "Lord, you've promised to surround me with favor (Psalm 5:12), now please give me favor with this man in this matter."

When he returned, I was relieved to learn that the tread of my tires had been worn just 9/32—so I was safely within the 1/3 limit. After some figuring, he offered, "I'm going to charge you just for the tread you've used on the four tires and replace them with new ones of a much better quality."

I expressed my sincere gratitude, but felt it wise to suppress my surprise and joy in realizing the generosity of his charging me only $52 for a set of tires selling for about $275! "Lord, this just had to be you again. You are touching earth again—and this time in the form of four beautiful tires. What a *Good Year* this ought to be!"

God Recycles **Broken** *Dreams*

Chapter 12
God's Pets, Too

It is a rather humbling experience to become aware that one has been ignorantly ignoring God's desire to be involved in a specific area of one's life. This happened to me in regard to our selection and care of animal pets. Until just recent years, we chose our pets rather at random—mostly as a result of our own whims. But how much more exciting and meaningful to consult the God of the whole animal kingdom; after all, he is the Creator!

When we moved to California, Bev wished aloud, "Mom, I wish we could have another black cat like Midnight."

"He was special to you wasn't he, Bev? It sure was sad to lose him." (How well I recalled having awakened one morning while living in Maine and seeing our much-loved pet stretched out on the highway, victim of a hit-and-run driver. I had gotten the help of my kind neighbor to help remove Midnight before Bev awoke to this sad sight).

"But, Bev," I continued, "how could we ever find another black kitten of a Siamese mother. That was a rather rare accident!"

"That's what made him special, Mom... that face that looked like a Siamese and even with a Siamese yowl!"

"Well, Bev, let's pray for God to help us find just the right kitten"... and for the first time, I actually recognized and expected God's interest in this very human matter of selecting a pet.

To demonstrate his appreciation for having been acknowledged for his interest in the animal kingdom, within ten days of that simple request, an ad appeared in the newspaper that read like this: "Kittens of Siamese mother—free, call ###."

I shared this with Bev and encouraged her to call. "If that mother cat has a black male kitten... he would have to be ours!"

Sure enough, in this litter of mixed breeds and colors, there was one black one, and it was a male. Within thirty minutes we had arrived at the owner's home and enjoyed watching this little lively family at play. We immediately spotted the only black one, but he engaged in the catch-me-if-you-can game, scampering about in the garage underneath a vehicle. He quickly earned the name "Rascal," which remained unchanged. Captured at last, he won our hearts without much added effort.

That evening it was with grateful hearts that we thanked God for fulfilling our wish so promptly and exactly as we asked. I could almost hear him say, *Really, this wasn't that hard for me to arrange. I keep an eye on what's going on with all my creatures.*

Such a rewarding experience gave me renewed hope to pray for a long-haired orange cat similar to one we had enjoyed about ten years previously. Before this new realization of involving God in the selection of a pet, I had responded to two different ads concerning orange kittens, but in each case they were disappointing disasters. The one actually was sick and the owner had not been honest in sharing the facts, so I had returned it. The other one just meowed day and night for over a week in loneliness for its mother and just would not adjust to his separation, so he also had to be returned.

But in God's timing, he arranged for a most beautiful, plush orange kitten to join our household. It all happened so easily. One day while my sister was visiting in the home of a Christian dentist, she observed their beautiful orange

God Recycles **Broken** *Dreams*

cat and immediately inquired, "Where did you ever get such a beautiful cat? My sister has been wanting one like that for several years!"

"My parents live on a farm near Santa Rosa," he explained, "and they have a mother cat that produces these lovely long-haired kittens quite often. The next time she has a litter, I'll let you know."

I could hardly wait for my order to be filled. I was especially grateful when I learned that our little kitten was the only one to have survived a particular litter of four because of a virus. It was love at first sight with this lovely, lively ball of orange and white fur. Because of her color and gingerly behavior, we named her Ginger.

Although Ginger received a warm welcome from Bev and me, it was quite in contrast to the arched, hissing resentment displayed by Rascal, apparently feeling that his private territory had been invaded. In spite of daily threats by Rascal, gentle Ginger maintained her winsomeness. At times, I would nick-name them Isaac and Ishmael, and threaten Bev that her cat (Rascal) Ishmael would have to be cast out of our household in order to have peace within our walls. But she disagreed, rather liking Rascal's spunkiness. He was a handsome creature with his sleek, velvety black coat and with those piercing yellow eyes.

In spite of Rascal's ornery nature, the Lord, too, evidenced his concern and love for Rascal. One Sunday evening, after having returned from church, while Bev and I were watching a musical on TV, I suddenly sensed a deep longing for Rascal, and said, almost with urgency, "Bev, call Rascal in."

She did, but there was no response. My feeling persisted, so I urged Bev to call for him again, but still no response. I insisted she keep calling for him until he responded. After the third call, Rascal came down over the ivy-covered bank in our backyard, across the yard and into our house. About ten minutes later, I just happened to glance out of our back window and there to my astonishment stood a wide-eyed raccoon only about six feet from our back door. A dangerous encounter between Rascal and this wild creature had been averted.

Rascal had been Bev's special buddy for five years at the time we were making plans to move from California to Florida. We realized that it would be almost impossible to bring either of our cats along on this extensive car trip, and even if that had been feasible, Rascal, being the roamer that he was, would not have been comfortable in the restriction of a mobile home in Florida. So we had to suffer the painful trauma of finding new homes for our precious pets. But God was interested in this phase also, and as we prayed for guidance for the right situation, a fine Christian school family who lived on a farm offered to take Rascal (what a tearful, yowling parting that was!)

As for Ginger, our good neighbors were happy to give her a new home, and even offered to send her to us by plane after our arrival in Florida. So after getting settled, I called Joyce. "Is your offer still good to put Ginger on the plane and send her this way? We sure do miss her!"

"Of course, Ruth, I'll be glad to. I'll make the necessary arrangements and call you back when I know the flight schedule." It is always exciting to go to an airport to meet a friend or relative, but this was the first time that we had gone to the airport to meet a golden, fluffy cat! I had prayed earlier that day before her departure from California for the Lord to delegate some special kitty angels to travel with her so that her flight might not be too frightening. And truly some force of love had surrounded her, for without any tranquilizer she arrived beautifully calm and even purring! How we praised God for this gift of love and for his tender care.

Not only have we witnessed God's guidance in the selection and care of our pet cats, but also in respect to a horse. Like many children, Bev was always excited over the sight of a horse. From a very young age she had the opportunity to ride a pony and then gradually, larger horses. But those limited thirty minutes or one-hour riding periods always left her sad and frustrated. It was such a temporary satisfaction.

God Recycles **Broken** *Dreams*

When we traveled across country at various times, Bev's father would make occasion to stop at a farm house to arrange for Bev and her traveling pal to have a horse ride. Once we happened to be in the Portland, Oregon area, where an annual crawfish festival was in progress. With horses being a feature of the parade and later at the gathering in the area park, Bev was given several opportunities to enjoy horse rides that day.

Whenever possible, we would attend horse shows and gymkhanas in various localities where we lived. But again, always looking over the fence and wishing she could be on the inside as part of the action was frustrating. I recall one such an occasion when spontaneously I spoke a word of faith, "Bev, it isn't always going to be this way, your being on the outside looking in. You're going to have a horse of your own, and some day be a part of a gymkhana yourself… and I feel that will be rather soon."

And indeed, after a prayerful search (and we do have to put legs on our prayers), we found a beauty—a ten-year-old albino mare, very gentle, yet with ample spirit when challenged. Dixie was a dream come true for Bev, and not a *nightm*are either!

Finding a reasonable and accessible boarding stable presented another challenge, but again we prayed for guidance, and as God has promised, "In all your ways acknowledge him, and he shall direct your path," He truly directed our steps to an ideal situation. Tormey Gardens, within six miles of our home, offered vast expanses of pasture lands and hills on which to ride, and also it was the site of the Bayview Horse Association gymkhanas. With these wonderful benefits, it was most gratifying for us to learn that the monthly boarding fee was just about half of the asking price of surrounding, less desirable stables. "Thank you, Father, for this gift of guidance!"

The overseer of Tormey Gardens, Vince, was another bonus with his competent alertness and willingness to give us advice in the proper care of

Dixie. One evening, Vince telephoned to inform us that he had removed a rusty nail from Dixie's right rear hoof and assured us that he had even administered a tetanus shot. Arriving at the scene, we observed her painful limping and felt her inflamed, swollen foot. Several bystanders shared tales of woe of how they had known horses with a similar injury, and now as a result, they could not be ridden for several months. One person pushed the panic button even more by relating an incident of a horse that had to be put to sleep because of the serious complications from this type of injury.

Although we very realistically had to reckon with the seriousness of Dixie's injury, I refused to absorb all these negative facts conveyed by well-meaning folk; my spirit simply rejected all these possible fearful consequences, and instead focused in on God's love for his animal kingdom. "Father," I prayed, "you know how many years Bev has desired a horse and now that you have helped us to get Dixie, I know you will help us in this dilemma. Now give us calmness of spirit and wisdom."

Recalling a childhood memory of my parents' using Epsom Salt as a "cure-all" for similar injuries, we purchased a large box from the nearby drugstore. As Bev gently soaked Dixie's rear foot in a bucket of Epsom Salt solution, I stroked Dixie's neck lovingly and prayed for God's healing love to flow through her foot. Repeating this treatment of Epsom Salt and prayer every day for several days, we were much encouraged to notice a diminishing of the swelling and heat in her hoof. By the fifth day, Dixie was able to walk without a limp and by the sixth day, she was actually running in the open field again. How we rejoiced and praised God! Those who had predicted woeful consequences commented, "You're sure lucky!"

Not only did our Creator God show his loving care for the creature Dixie, but also in his mercy spared Bev from what could have been a major catastrophe early that memorable morning in May. Because of the intense afternoon heat

God Recycles **Broken** *Dreams*

during that time of the year, I had offered to take Bev and her friend Gail out to exercise Dixie early that morning before school started.

So while the girls were out in the field with Dixie, I remained in the car— just reflecting on the beauty of the morning while I read Psalm 46 as part of my devotional reading for that morning. Suddenly my joyful spirit of praise to God seemed to become very heavy, and for no good reason, it seemed. I found myself crying out to God, "Oh God, protect us this day with your canopy of love. Cover us with your blood."

My mind, striving for an interpretation of this sudden heaviness of heart, envisioned some possible danger later that day at our school where I was responsible for about 150 children. Little did I realize that right at that time, Bev and Gail had been thrown off Dixie's back. Evidently resenting the discomfort of being ridden double, Dixie bucked, thereby throwing both the girls to the ground with a thud, and then tried to escape to the far end of the extended field. Bev, although in shock, realized Dixie should not be allowed the get-even spirit of a runaway—especially not with valuable bridle and reins dangling—so she pursued intently.

Glancing at my watch uneasily and realizing the girls should have returned to the car by this time, I started out looking for them. Unable to catch sight of them anywhere in the wide open fields, I felt fear grip my spirit. Just about then I saw them coming around the bend, trudging rather strangely, leading Dixie along. As they came into closer view, I noticed Gail's flushed, frightened look and Bev's shockingly pale white face covered with beads of perspiration.

"What happened?" I queried anxiously.

"We were thrown off the horse," Gail responded, almost tearfully.

"Are you hurt?" was my next quick concern.

"My head hurts, but I'll be alright," Gail answered.

Bev was strangely quiet.

"Let's get in the car. I feel I should have you both checked out at the hospital."

As I drove along rapidly, I noticed Bev holding her right arm as though it were hurting. Within a short time, we were in the emergency room of Doctors Hospital. Gail checked out okay, much to my relief. But Bev had managed to break the humerus bone in her right arm at the shoulder joint. She was in increasing pain and distress. The following day, she was scheduled for surgery and then fitted with a most grotesque cast which required her right arm to be extended straight outward from her shoulder with a waist cast with staves as props from the waist up to her arm cast. In those anxious hours, I reread Psalm 46, especially verse one. "God is our refuge and strength, a tested help in times of trouble."

With such a clumsy contraption of a cast, Bev invariably received the second look from passers-by, whether on the street or at school. Often these curious ones would ask Bev, "How do you ever sleep with that thing?"

Not having lost her sense of humor with her fall, she retorted quickly, "I don't stay awake to find out!"

Teasingly, I accused her of resembling the Statue of Liberty with her outstretched arm: an unplanned, but perhaps appropriate celebration during our country's bicentennial year of 1976.

Bev and Dixie continued their friendship, especially after Bev learned to respect Dixie's likes and dislikes a little more carefully. After six weeks of wearing her cast, she was relieved of it and ready to ride Dixie again.

The following year as plans were developing for our move to Florida, I prayed for the Lord to somehow gradually wean Bev from her good friend Dixie so that parting would not be overly painful. Indeed, that is just what happened; other interests increasingly absorbed her time. We were very

God Recycles **Broken** *Dreams*

concerned, however, that kind, competent hearts and hands would become Dixie's new owners.

It was the very morning of our moving day that a fine couple purchased our horse. Watching their skillful handling of Dixie and listening to their sound attitudes toward animals, we felt we had entrusted Dixie into the care of friends. Having received updates on Dixie, we were grateful for God's guidance in this matter, too. Wise Solomon observed, "A good man is concerned for the welfare of his animals, but even the kindness of godless men is cruel" (Proverbs 12:10).

Reviewing the involvement of God in a very intimate, caring way with our much-loved pets seems to make my God closer than ever before. But as I reflected upon this whole sphere of God's concern, I smilingly realized that this was not at all a new interest from God's point of view. It was rather an awakening of my own awareness of his ongoing care from ages past.

Was not God very much involved in the creation of all the animals, fish, and birds—as recorded in the first chapter of Genesis? Then was not Jesus' earthly life surrounded by these creatures in every important phase of his life? At birth, he was given the warmth and manger of the animals in the stable; and even before his advent, it was a donkey that carried his mother to Bethlehem as she was "great with child." At Jesus' baptism, the Holy Spirit descended upon him in the form of a dove. Then in his teaching he often referred to his animal friends: the sheep, goats, dogs, foxes, and birds, in order to convey spiritual lessons. Was not Jesus involved in assisting his weary disciples to make an unforgettable catch of fish? As part of his triumphal entry into Jerusalem, he rode upon a donkey. A cock crowing was the reminder to Peter of his denial of the Lord. Jesus was referred to as "the Lamb of God" by John the Baptist, and in Revelation, as "...the Lion of the tribe of Judah." Yes, God the Father, and Jesus Christ, his Son, have been very much involved with the animal kingdom!

When children ask searchingly, "Will there be animals in Heaven?" my humble response is "Of course!" Many centuries ago Isaiah, through his inspired telescope, caught a glimpse of the new earth and kingdom of God as it shall be:

"In that day the wolf and the lamb will lie down together, and the leopard and goats will be at peace. Calves and fat cattle will be safe among lions, and a little child shall lead them all. The cows will graze among bears; cubs and calves will lie down together, and lions will eat grass like the cows. Babies will crawl safely among poisonous snakes, and a little child who puts his hand in a nest of deadly adders will pull it out unharmed. Nothing will hurt or destroy in all my holy mountain, for as the waters fill the sea, so shall the earth be full of the knowledge of the Lord" (Isaiah 11:6-9).

"Thank you, Father, for your love and concern for our animal friends; help us never to be abusive toward them, but rather instruments of your care."

God Recycles Broken Dreams

Chapter 13
Principal's Parish

What an exhausting day it had been with its unending demands, starting with the early eight o'clock faculty business meeting and devotions, then counseling the distraught mother who felt her daughter had been mistreated on the playground, suspending Jerry for repeated cheating, comforting a mother whose home life was almost intolerable, listening to the photographer's new offer for school pictures, prayer with a parent whose father was facing open-heart surgery, and strengthening a parent who shared a temptation in her new Christian walk. Feeling the need of a little relaxation, I took my lunch break at my mother's house; but I found she also was in need of some assurance, having received a well-intended letter which she had misinterpreted. Then back to my desk where there was a stack of incoming mail awaiting my attention before my appointment with our athletic coach. "Oh, there goes the buzzer—that's right, we did schedule a fire drill for this afternoon!"

By the time I returned to my office, our guest speaker for chapel was waiting for me. When dismissal time arrived, I still had quite a few unfinished tasks that needed my attention before I could leave.

Knock, knock. "I wonder who needs me now?" I thought to myself quite impatiently. "Come in," I invited, trying to muster up a pleasant voice.

And in burst two lively kindergarten girls leading still another one who had been hurt during their after-school child-care playtime.

"Mrs. Shank, please pray for Krissy. She hurt her back when she fell out there," one of them explained.

After a little examination, I felt she was really all right, but to pacify the concerned ones we did have prayer. Then they came back several more times within a short time span, with such requests as, "Please pray for my uncle, for my grandfather..."

Realizing that while they were flourishing on all this special attention, I was being unnecessarily depleted, so I called a halt by saying quite sternly, "Girls, you cannot come back again to my office this afternoon. You've already been in here four times, and I have lots of work to get done today."

Charlene, the spokesman, looked up so innocently at me and responded very soberly, "Can we come back seven times?" and catching my disapproving look, she compromised quickly with, "Can we come back tomorrow?"

Realizing "tomorrow" would be Saturday, I answered with relief, "All right, but no more today!"

Temporarily pacified, this winsome threesome opened my office door to leave when Charlene, not to be denied a last request urged, "Can we pray for God?"

Smiling to myself, I thought as busy as we keep him, perhaps he could use some prayer, too!

El Sobrante Christian School in California was opened in September 1971 with just eleven pupils but with a vision to reinstate the three basic R's--Reading, 'Riting, and 'Rithmetic and with the fourth added dimension of Respect, which has become a lost value in many public classrooms. This respect was based upon the summary of God's law, "Thou shalt love the Lord thy God with all thy heart and with all thy soul and with all thy mind and thy neighbor as thyself" (Matthew 22:37,39 KJV), which fosters respect for God, oneself, and for others.

God Recycles **Broken** *Dreams*

With this Christian philosophy, our school experienced a continuous, healthy growth, expanding from kindergarten through junior high level. Academically, our pupils, even though many had come to us with deplorable deficiencies in reading and math skills, invariably averaged, with few exceptions, well above national norms on the annual Stanford Achievement Tests. For several years our first grade class scored a fourth grade equivalency—quite a stark contrast to the many published reports of below par achievement scores in our public school scene.

With all due respect to those administrators and conscientious teachers in the public school system who are trying to get the job done right, it is an inexcusable crime that we in the United States are spending more money for education than all other countries of the world combined, and yet with correspondingly less results. In fact, it has been estimated that there are over twenty million functionally illiterate persons over 18 years of age living in the United States—what a tragic commentary on our educational system!

For one of my newspaper ads advertising our school, I had a doughnut sketched with this challenging question: Is your child suffering from doughnut education—with the center missing? That center was explained as being God, for truly unless he is at the center of our thinking, learning and behaving, everything is out of balance. Many people are oblivious of the truth, "The fear of the Lord is the beginning of knowledge" (Proverbs 1:7 KJV).

Not only did we stress God as the center of our learning and lives—teaching our pupils that God not only created this complex and marvelous universe, but he also sustains it by his laws of operation—we also recognized God's Word as the stable bedrock of authority for our social behavior. When Billy was sent into my office for repeated offenses of kicking his fellow classmates while sitting in the kindergarten reading circle, I reminded him, "Billy, you know that when you kick any boy or girl in your class, you are kicking God's child!" That was an awesome thought for Billy.

There was the incident where several third-grade boys thought it was smart and even "grown-up" to indulge in dirty body language. I informed them that whenever they spoke of their body disrespectfully, they were actually making fun of something God had made; and just as they would feel insulted if someone made fun of something they made, so God was injured by their making fun of their bodies. Also to reinforce this lesson, I had these students memorize appropriate scripture verses, such as, "Dirty stories, foul talk, and coarse jokes, these are not for you—Instead, remind each other of God's goodness and be thankful" (Ephesians 5:4).

I recall two sixth-grade boys being sent into my office by the playground supervisor during lunch recess. Steve and Joe were fighting mad! One had grabbed the basketball from the other one, and name-calling with a fight ensued. (Yes, all this even at a Christian school... aren't children everywhere thoroughly human—and with no apology!) So as they entered my office, and with a quick appraisal of the situation that they both were guilty of misbehavior, I broke the angry silence with, "Steve and Joe, looks to me like you are enemies right now. We won't waste time discussing how it all came about, but what are we going to do about it? Perhaps looking at Jesus Christ would help us to know what to do; after all, he had enemies quite often. Can you fellows recall what Jesus did with his enemies?"

"I suppose he forgave them," Steve offered quite begrudgingly.

"Well, that's true," I agreed, "but he did even more than that. Do you remember when he hung on the cross that he even prayed for the very enemies who had nailed him there? That must have been hard to do, don't you think? I really think, Steve and Joe, it would please God very much for you two to pray for each other—and probably even before you do that, we ought to have a few moments of silent prayer to ask God to cleanse our hearts from all hate and anger."

After a few moments of silent prayer, I asked Steve to pray for Joe and then Joe for Steve. Those boyish confessions must have blessed the heart of God,

God Recycles **Broken** *Dreams*

"Please, God, help me not to lose my temper so fast the next time; I'm sorry I got so mad at Joe. Please help him, too."

Within a few minutes, they were shaking hands as friends and left my office smiling. Yes, Jesus Christ came down to earth to teach boys and girls how to handle their everyday problems.

Speaking of girls, they had their problems in social behavior, too. Sally and Sue had each come to my office independently to tell on the other. So I called them both into the office together. Obviously partly ashamed and also still pouting it out against each other, they refused to look at each other. I stood up between them and putting an arm around each of them, I said to them, "I love you girls very much and best of all, Jesus loves you."

I heard sobbing from Sue, and Sally's eyes were misty, too. Without any more words, they reached over and hugged each other. God's love had come through, and that heals all broken relationships.

To watch the spiritual growth of these precious children and youth was perhaps one of the most enriching experiences of my own life. This was nurtured by opening every class with prayer, and actually involving the pupils with their needs and having them pray for each other. Also, every day each class had its Bible lesson as part of the curriculum with emphasis on Bible memorization; how thrilling it was to hear individuals and classes recite complete chapters and Psalms. My greatest dream was to have Psalm 119 with its entire 176 verses recited, and that was accomplished by each class reciting a section of it—what an unforgettable experience! On another occasion, the entire student body sang Psalm 150. Then there were the weekly chapel times when we would gather together in the beautiful sanctuary to worship God in music, prayer, and with a visualized Bible lesson. There were also the Spiritual Emphasis Weeks when we met every day for a series of Bible lessons on such themes as "God's Family," sharing with our pupils about the various Bible families with all their problems of anger, hate, murder, jealousies, and also how God's love and forgiveness was available. Many students responded to the challenge to become members of the Christian family through Jesus Christ. Once when giving a series on the Lordship of Jesus Christ, I prefaced a lesson by asking, "Why do children need Jesus to be their Lord, perhaps we should just wait until we get older?" An alert 8-year-old Stephen replied with tremendous earnestness, "We would just go plain crazy if we didn't have Jesus!"

Stephen was blessed with Christian parents, but we also ministered to many children from non-Christian homes. What a joy it was to see many of these for the first time in their lives be confronted with the claims of Jesus Christ. There was Daryl, whose mother was an alcoholic and whose father had other problems. Although the parents were not Christians, they were aware of their son's inability to get along with others and consequently had moved to our location specifically to enroll Daryl in our school. Because of unresolved home problems, Daryl's temper and frustrations were at the breaking point much of the time. After patient, repeated counseling and prayer with and for Daryl, we watched him gradually become rooted in the life and teachings of Jesus Christ in a beautiful, victorious way. After one of those frequent sessions in my office, Daryl prayed, "Dear God, I want to thank you that I can come here to talk to Mrs. Shank. She helps me more than anyone I know. And I thank you for this wonderful school where I can learn so much about you."

I often put my hand on Daryl's shoulder and reminded him, "From the very first day you came here, Daryl, I felt you were very special to God. Keep close to him and he will use you. I wonder if he might not lead you to become a minister!"

Many of our pupils came from broken homes. One day little Karen came to me tearfully, "I want to see my real Daddy," she sobbed.

Realizing that her stepfather, although kind to her, was having some problems of his own, I drew Karen close to me and asked gently, "How long has it been since you've seen your real Daddy, Karen?"

God Recycles **Broken** *Dreams*

"I don't know, but it's been a long time and I want to see him." Aware that her father lived about 500 miles from her home, I suggested, "Let's pray together, Karen, because God, our heavenly Father, loves you very much and I know your Daddy loves you, too; so let's pray that God will somehow talk to your Daddy and let him know you want to see him."

We prayed and God heard Karen's heart cry, for before that week ended, her Daddy had called by phone and made arrangements for her to spend the following weekend with him.

A heart-wrenching scene forever etched on my mind was that of a third-grade boy standing between his sorrowful mother and her estranged husband who had developed an interest in another woman. The father had just come home to inform his Korean war-bride of former years that he no longer loved her and wanted a divorce. But here stood Harold pleading with his father at the doorway leading to his classroom, "Dad, I'm not going to class unless you promise to stay with us. I want you to be there when I get home from school today!"

Finally after many agonizing moments and pleas, the father at least consented to stay until Harold got home from school that day. So after Harold had gone to his classroom, I invited this estranged couple into my office. Any effort for reconciliation seemed futile at that point, but later the mother did stop by several times for counsel and encouragement during her traumatic period of readjustment.

"Oh, Jesus, you who looked upon the wandering multitudes with great compassion, as sheep having no shepherd, now how your heart must grieve for these little lambs whose spirits are bleating!"

Yes, I gradually discovered that my principalship of this Christian day school entailed much more than developing the curriculum, ordering textbooks, interviewing and testing pupils, hiring teachers, and conducting staff meetings—I found I was ministering to flesh and blood, hurting, needy human beings. It was not unusual to have five or six parents waiting outside my office door after school, desiring to share with me their financial, emotional, physical or other family problems. I was challenged to do my "homework" early each morning before ever arriving at school by feeding on God's promises. I find it is only as we ourselves first digest spiritual food that we are able to feed other hungry hearts. This beautiful scripture was meaningful to me: "The Lord God has given me his words of wisdom so that I may know what I should say to all these weary ones. Morning by morning, he wakens me and opens my understanding to his will" (Isaiah 50:4).

Hearing the needs and struggles of parents challenged me to conduct several series of parent seminars in which we discussed the various facets of family relationships and child rearing. With the aid of several good textbooks, such as *Help, I'm a Parent!*, by Bruce Narramore and *Dare to Discipline* by James Dobson, together with the Bible and principles of Christian psychology, we were able to outline very practical methods of effective wholesome discipline for children. As part of the evaluation of these sessions, parents would comment gratefully, "I'm much calmer, less frustrated now in handling my children..." "I can discipline without guilt feelings..." "My child is much more loving and loveable..." "Our home is changed from chaos and confusion to peace and tranquility—how we love it!" "We only regret we didn't have this course 20 years ago!" These changed lives and homes were gratifying to me, indeed.

There were also numerous social occasions during a school year that drew our school family together in fun, food, and fellowship—like the annual Thanksgiving dinner and program during which time the pupils presented skits, songs and readings in traditional costumes. What inspiring Christmas and Easter programs were presented by the students to a capacity audience of over five hundred parents and friends. Then there was that rousing patriotic Bicentennial celebration with the red, white and blue banners flying while students sang, "Fifty, Nifty United States," (naming all the states in alphabetical

God Recycles Broken Dreams

sequence) and "The Presidents Song" (composed by one of our teachers, Betty Hendrickson, listing all the presidents of the United States in chronological order). Who could ever forget the home-made ice cream with fresh strawberries festival, and the International Festival, with those aromatic food booths representing various countries and the pupils in corresponding costumes with songs of other lands. Whoever said school couldn't be fun!

As I reflect upon this tremendous segment of my life, I realize it could never have been possible without the fantastic staff God put together—truly like handpicked fruit. A school can be only as good as its teachers, and what a committed, dedicated, talented group we had. There was B. J. with her cheerful whistle every morning and "It's going to be all right" no matter the problem; Mary—rather than retire, she was retread for much more productive mileage with those eager kindergarteners; Diane—teaching her little ones much more than just ABC's with her culinary skills; sensitive, perceptive Betty D.—caring for each pupil as though her very own; Paula and Jean, sharing so many common interests besides their excellent teaching of first graders—such as identical wedding dates and skiing honeymoons; Betty H., a good "old-fashioned" teacher who let her fifth graders know what grammar and long division were all about; Debby—a most creative bundle of ceaseless ideas and wife of a supportive, seminary student; and Pat—the motherly one with the ability to get our band started. Then there was David, a stable leader and model for our junior highers; and Morris and Joyce, our dependable day-care supervisors and associate teachers; Vivian, our faithful and capable secretary with Verna, as competent treasurer and Pastor Robert Sinner (we just never did get him converted!), as caring Captain of our crew.

As a staff, we laughed and cried together. I will always remember the time one of our part-time teachers was trying to get the class pulled together just after they had come back from recess. In an attempt to get their attention, he blew his whistle; but to his added aggravation, in an instant, all the students were beneath their desks! He wondered what kind of pranks they were up to until someone explained meekly that their regular classroom teacher gave them disaster drills by blowing her whistle signaling them to find cover under their desks. Whose face was red now! There were also times of understanding and misunderstanding, of grievances and cleansings, but we all stretched and grew in our relationship to God and to each other.

We learned the rewards of "honesty is the best policy," and "speaking the truth in love" (Ephesians 4:15), rather than harboring a grievance against another. For the truth sets us free, whereas unresolved grudges fester and poison the whole stream of relationships. Periodically, pressures seemed to build up to a boil, but as we humbled ourselves and sought to understand each other, a beautiful inner cleansing and healing would take place. God's love can only flow through unobstructed vessels and it is worth everything to keep the channels open.

Our regular early morning staff devotions were the highlight of each day as teachers shared diversified inspirational thoughts. For one school year opener, we used the challenge, "Keep Looking Down!" based upon Ephesians 1:14 and 2:16. No matter what problems we might encounter, we should always take our position in Christ *above* the problem and not get buried beneath them. To be sure, we had to remind one another of this concept frequently as the cares and concerns would accumulate. It was always good to get back up there where we belonged.

Our staff devotions also involved a prayer and praise notebook in which we recorded the needs of our school family and of others as we became aware of them, and as these prayer requests were answered, we would record the "thank-you's," like; job for Kenny's father, Ginny's grandfather's surgery, spiritual needs of Bill's family, etc. What a joy it was to be partners together with God in these matters.

We had moments of holy laughter, too, as when we prayed one morning for special protection for two classes that were planning to go on field trips that

God Recycles **Broken** *Dreams*

day. "Please, Father, dispatch extra angels to flutter all around these children"... and before I could finish, we all burst out in amused laughter... then I tried to continue, "but please, Father, don't send them *all* along on those field trips because we need some of them here on our school playground, too."

The teachers went to their classes with merry hearts that morning.

Speaking of angels, I must digress to share the adorable experiences we had as I distributed angel passes to the kindergarten and primary teachers during a particular Christmas season. These passes were in the shape of angels, with the words written on them, "I'm a Christmas Angel," and were to be given to a child who did something worthy of recognition in the regular classroom procedure. Then they would come to my office with this angel pass and would have the privilege of taking a candy cane off a little felt tree I had in my office. Just any time during those two weeks, I could expect a little angel to come flitting into my office, to which I would inquire, "And what did you do to be an angel?"

These were some of the darling replies:

"I helped my teacher pick up stars."

"I didn't complain all day."

"I forgot." (I didn't know angels could forget).

"I sing good."

"I was a good rester at naptime."

"I don't know." (Angels must be human, too)!

"I waited for my turn."

As one was leaving my office, I cautioned her not to lose the candy cane which had been taped to her angel pass, to which she replied wistfully, "No, then I'd have to be another angel."

Not only were our staff members sincerely concerned about the welfare of our school family, but we also had an active prayer committee, comprised of parents who each day faithfully prayed for each pupil and staff member. This was a beautiful reciprocation of sharing and caring in prayer.

Often we would pray for special equipment or material needs for our school. Within a few days after we had talked to the Lord about some much needed playground equipment, another principal called me from out-of-town to inform me that a park in his area was dismantling all their play-ground equipment and we were able to obtain about one thousand dollars worth of items for less than two hundred. In another instance, our fourth grade teacher had expressed her need for a set of encyclopedias for her class-room. Within the same week, there was an ad in the local paper listing a twenty-volume set of new encyclopedias with a two-volume dictionary, large atlas, and a ten-volume set of classic literature; all this listed for $365, but the party would sell for $150. In checking with our administrator, we agreed that it would be nice to get them for just $100, because of our limited budget. And that is exactly what happened. When the seller learned the books would be used in our school, he offered the low price of $100! Also, periodically God would send to us a wonderful person, Ray Schuler, with a truckload of outdoor play furniture, bookcases, tables—all free and made by him—as a ministry of love to God's little ones.

So God was very much involved in every aspect of our school; in fact, I reminded him quite often that it was actually his school, and he was the Super-vising Principal, for surely without him, I would have perished in my parish! There were many times I felt that the load of stresses and demands were more than I could humanly carry, and they truly were; but at such times, the Holy Spirit would very tenderly remind me, "They that wait upon the Lord shall renew their strength. They shall mount up with wings like eagles; they shall run and not be weary; they shall walk and not faint" (Isaiah 40:31).

God Recycles Broken Dreams

Also, I was encouraged with, "This is my work, and I can do it only because Christ's mighty energy is at work within me" (Colossians 1:29).

Once again, I learned that to the extent I was willing to die to my own desires and ways, to that measure God's new life could flow through our school in vitalizing force. Parents and even salesmen would observe, "What is it about this school? I feel something here."

I would let them know assuredly, "This is God's presence and where he is, there is love. That's what you feel."

There were innumerable expressions of God's love among us. Our staff poured this love into the minds and hearts of our pupils every day in innumerable ways. We instilled in their hearts the message that each of them was uniquely a VIP to God and to us and the world. That no one else could fulfill their individual assignment in life. We would especially impart this love to the shattered, frightened ones of our students, like little blond Cindy. She frequently witnessed her mother and father in physical fights and abuse, and consequently, was like a frightened little fawn. Feeling so insecure led her to stealing—crayons, barrettes and whatever she could confiscate from her classmates. After her teacher was stymied in not knowing how to handle this unresolved behavior, she sent Cindy to my office with this note, "She did it again. I just don't know what more to do. Please help!"

Reasoning told me that Cindy needed to be disciplined for this habit of stealing, but as I quickly sent up a silent S.O.S. for guidance, the answer came back gently, "Just love her."

So I took Cindy up on my lap and held her rigid, fearful body close to me. Tenderly, I spoke, "Cindy, do you know that Mrs. Shank loves you very much, and your teacher loves you very much, and best of all, Jesus loves you very much."

This infusion of love opened up the fountains of tears within her bottled-up heart, and soon she was sobbing softly. Then we prayed a prayer of forgiveness for her stealing. Before sending her back to her class with instructions to ask forgiveness of the child from whom she had stolen, I admonished her, "Cindy, you don't have to steal from anyone again; if there is something you really need and we can give it to you, we will, because remember, we really do love you."

The next morning in our staff devotions, I encouraged all the teachers to be alert and seek for opportunity on the playground or elsewhere to assure Cindy and also her brother, Alex, of our love. Within weeks they were truly transformed into radiant, loving youngsters—running to us with outstretched arms of love. They had been the recipients of God's love. The sequel to that story is that months later their dear mother, a very intelligent person yet pursuing all kinds of wrong paths for truth, stopped in my office to pour out her grief and hurts. "Elizabeth," I urged, "if you would yield to God and let him be Lord in your life, it would be so much different."

And that is what she did and became a glowing believer in Jesus Christ. I learned later that each evening, Elizabeth, with Cindy and Alex, would kneel for bedtime prayers and the children would ask, "Please help Daddy to stop drinking and love you, too."

"Lord, thank you for allowing me to minister in such a precious parish. Truly, you taught, "Anyone who takes care of a little child like this is caring for me! And whoever cares for me is caring for God who sent me" (Luke 9:48).

God Recycles **Broken** *Dreams*

Chapter 14
Year of Jubilee

Birthdays are special occasions and celebrated in a variety of ways. I know of companies that give their employees a holiday from work on their birthday; what a nice personal gift! I have enjoyed innumerable happy surprises on my birthdays—I shall always remember that 16th surprise party at which I was given a beautiful light blue musical powder box designed with pink roses which tinkled with the romantic tune, "Moonlight and Roses." Then on the 49th all my pupils and staff hid in our lunch room until I returned from my lunch break and then burst out into singing, "Happy Birthday." They gave me gifts, cards and many smiles. But on January 23, 1977, I had the most special one of all—my 50th! When at the breakfast table I said with a sobering chuckle, "Happy birthday to me—for the 50th time." Bev, my young 16-year-old, burst my balloon with, "Wow, Mom, 50! That sounds ancient!" Fortunately that was a Sunday, and after church dear Mrs. Ratcliff, a 96-year-old saint, came up to me with her big smile and said, "Ruthie, I hear it's your birthday today. How old are you?"

Realizing how well she had weathered the 96 winters of her life, I gained courage and answered without apology and matter-of-factly, "50," to which she replied in a wistful way, "Oh, 50... that's so young!"

I preferred her interpretation to that of Bev's, you can be sure!

But this was to be a very special year, and probably due partly to the fact that I had decided and stated beforehand that this would be my "Year of Jubilee!" Didn't the Bible teach that every 50th year was to be so named, and should be very special in that it was heralded in by the blowing of the trumpets, and liberty was to be proclaimed throughout all the land to all enslaved debtors, and that it was a time for cancellation of all public and private debts? It was to be a year of cessation of labor and a restoration of family estates (Leviticus 25). My personal application of this special celebration was summarized in a stated desire to become liberated from all unnecessary material and financial entanglements, to have a year off from the pressures of having to earn a living and be free to travel, write and share Jesus Christ. In a most amazing way, all this was fulfilled. Didn't God say he would do "…exceeding, abundantly above all that we ask or think, according to the power that works in us" (Ephesians 3:20)?

The wheels started turning in March of that special year when I had a sense of "Mission Completed" in my fifth year as teacher/principal of the Christian day school in California. I had had the satisfaction of helping to make possible a 300% increase in growth from its early inception, and not only had it grown numerically but also in solidarity of operational policies and spiritual and academic excellence. Like many other worthy accomplishments, this feat was realized only through a painful process of grueling problems. Yet, at the completion of this five-year assignment, I experienced that wonderful sense of exhilarating reward—a job well done! Had I left sooner, I might have been running away from problems, but now with each problem having been worked through, I felt free in my spirit to submit my resignation to our school board. Although I appreciated the kindness of the board in their reluctance to accept my resignation, I reminded them, "I know the Lord is telling me my assignment is completed here, and to stay beyond his timing would be detrimental for me personally, as well as for the further progress of the school."

Upon my resignation, the most frequently asked question from staff and friends was, "Ruth, where are you going? Do you have another position?" "I

God Recycles **Broken** *Dreams*

really have no idea where I'll be going; all I can say is that I find myself in a position of joyous expectation!"

Didn't God, my Father, promise me, "For I know the plans I have for you, says the Lord. They are plans for good and not for evil, to give you a future and a hope" (Jeremiah 29:11).

Desiring to have all our school records in shipshape order for the incoming principal, I worked doubly hard—not only bringing the current school year to a thorough completion, but also handling many orders and interviews in preparation for a smooth transition for the succeeding school year. In the midst of this dual load, I would keep sending memos up to the Lord. "Now, Lord, you can see I'm very busy working for you here at my office, so I'm just trusting you to be working for me."

He replied with his assuring memo, "For since the world began no one has seen or heard of such a God as ours, who works for those who wait for him" (Isaiah 64:4).

During this time of working and waiting, one of our very precious young teachers shared with me that her husband, a ministerial candidate, had sent out about one hundred resumés.

"Wow," I thought, "I haven't sent out even one. Perhaps I ought to take some initiative in seeking a place and position, too."

But it was almost as if God had to slap my hands in each pursuit. As I proceeded to investigate opportunities in southern California, everything seemed to deadlock within my spirit as well as in circumstances. I even missed a particular flight, and consequently, a special appointment, which was the first time in all my life I had ever missed a plane; surely, this was not just a happenstance. Then when I pursued another prospect in a thriving church-school situation north of us, nothing sparked my spirit there; in fact, quite to the contrary, I nearly fell asleep on two separate visits in the services there, which again was a rare experience for me. I know and believe that we must endeavor to answer our own prayers as much as possible… put legs on our prayers… "ask, seek and knock…" But somehow in this phase of my life, God wanted to show me he could handle this matter very capably without my interference; and indeed, he did.

Shortly after having submitted my resignation as principal, I also listed and sold our little home with most of our furnishings. A friend asked me searchingly, "Isn't it kind of scary to sell everything and not even know where you're going?"

That was an honest question, and if I would have allowed myself to indulge in mere human ponderings, I would have been overwhelmed by anxiety and fear. But instead, I kept walking through the Word of God, stepping firmly on God's promises as though they were firm patio stones laid out amidst the uneven sands; such promises as "The people of the Lord will live where they are sent" (Micah 2:5); "… Your King will go before you—the Lord leads on" (Micah 2:13). The peace and joy of the Holy Spirit quieted my spirit—that is, until the weekend of anguish in May.

How fittingly that it should be on Mother's Day weekend that God should choose to work within my spirit to give birth to his new plan for me. Those who have been mothers, giving birth to a new life, understand the pangs of birth in this process of new life. My soul was gripped with such deep anguish that I hardly knew what was happening—which, indeed, intensified the distress. I recall having felt very heavy-hearted all that preceding Saturday, but by Sunday, I was really in labor—suffering sharp pangs within my spirit. I recall how I did not want to go to my own church that morning, nor did I want to see any familiar faces—not even my mother or sister. I had to face this struggle alone with God. I did visit a different church that morning, but felt very miserable, and could hardly wait for the benediction. I took Bev home with the instructions, "Bev, help

God Recycles **Broken** *Dreams*

yourself to food in the refrigerator. I'm not hungry, and I have to get away to be alone with the Lord."

Knowing that just being around water has a quieting, refreshing effect upon me, I drove over the beautiful San Rafael Bridge with the Bay waters on either side, and then over into attractive Marin County with its exquisite civic center, situated adjacent to a lovely man-made lake. I parked the car there and walked the full circuit around that lake—almost oblivious to the happy children trying to attract the ducks with offerings of potato chips and crusts of bread left over from their family picnic lunches. As I walked, my heart cried out to God in anguish, reaching up to him for direction, for relief, and for an explanation of what was happening. As I returned to the car, I wept almost uncontrollably. I didn't even know why. As I crossed over the Golden Gate Bridge, homeward bound from San Francisco, I noticed rain misting on my windshield almost as if Mother Nature were weeping with me.

By the time I arrived back home, something amazing transpired—I experienced a sudden wonderful relief. Truly like the moment of birth of a new life, and instantly, my whole inner spirit was diffused with a burst of Sonshine—with such warmth and inner glow. Out of the midst of this inner glow, I became very intensely aware of FLORIDA—almost like these bright rays within my spirit were pointing to Florida! It burst upon my consciousness that this was where God desired me to go for my next assignment. What really overwhelmed me was that I was so happy over this prospect because I never would have chosen to go to Florida. I had lived there in the 60's during which time I had learned that the high relative humidity, roaches and all the other flying and crawling creatures that inhabit the semi-tropical climates, were all very incompatible with my nature! But here I was, happy with anticipation of going back to Florida—this had to be God! As I went inside our home, trying to conceal my ecstasy, I asked Bev rather casually, "Bev, how would you feel about moving to Florida?" to which she responded just as casually, but with a light spirit, "Sounds good!"

I believe when parents follow God in obedience to his will, the children will also be content… unless they are willfully fighting God. "The humble shall see their God at work for them. No wonder they will be so glad! All who seek for God shall live in joy" (Psalm 69:32).

I wondered afterwards if all that striving and anguish could have been part of the struggles of dying to my own personal preferences and also to the closeness of family and friends in California. Whatever it all meant (and why should we even try to understand God's ways with us), I continued to listen to God's instructions. As I pondered Florida, it dawned upon me that I had received a letter from Dr. Robert Schuller's office of the Hour of Power TV program from southern California several weeks prior to this time, informing me that he planned on starting a sister church in Orange County, Florida. How well I recall when I first received that piece of mail saying, "Well, God, I'll sure pray for that new work, for workers to be sent there, but please don't count on me to go there!" How often we have to eat our bold statements!

So before retiring for a peaceful sleep that night, I searched through my backlog of correspondence on my desk and found that particular card which informed me that this new church was to be built in Zellwood, Florida. Whoever heard of Zellwood?! Seeking out our atlas, I finally located this small town north of Orlando. Now, at least, I knew where I was going.

Early the next morning I dialed the operator to ask for the Zellwood Chamber of Commerce. The Florida operator laughingly explained, "Zellwood doesn't have a Chamber of Commerce, but I can give you Apopka, which is nearby." In a few moments I was in conversation with a very buoyant, happy-to-be-living-in-Apopka kind of lady.

"Do you plan to become a part of the new Rolling Hills Community Church in Zellwood?" was the surprising question she asked me.

"Well, I'm not sure," I proceeded cautiously, "but I would like to know more about it and the area there."

God Recycles **Broken** *Dreams*

She responded with all kinds of helpful information, especially by giving me the name and address of Jim Doan, the business administrator who had come on ahead to get this new church on the road.

As I drove to school that morning, my head was in a tailspin. "Lord," I prayed, "I can hardly fathom what all has transpired this weekend, but if this is really you and this is your voice of direction, just let me continue to sense your wonderful, assuring peace," which is God's seal of approval. That beautiful peace of God with expectant joy just remained right there in the weeks to follow. "I will keep on expecting you to help me. I praise you more and more" (Psalm 71:14).

So for the next six weeks we were packing, selling our home and furniture, and meeting all the many demands of closing up a school year. Then there were all those emotion-packed moments of farewell—like receiving this darling note from one of the first graders:

"To Mrs. Shank from Jerome,

I love you Mrs. Shank. I wish you wont move. I wish you will stil be are Principal nesx yer. God bles you allwes to be Happy where ever you go. be Happy at florada but we will miss you."

There were many tokens of love from students' parents—one mother who had crocheted a set of lovely clothes hangers wrote on the accompanying card:

"These took so little time compared with all the time you've spent for my children. I want to thank you for all the love, patience and understanding that you've shown.

Love in Him, The Peronas."

The Parent Teacher Fellowship presented me with a beautiful garnet birthstone and diamond ring, and the kind school board gave generous gifts, including an impressive walnut and marble desk pen set with inscription, "In appreciation for faithful service." Among the most painful severances was the one between our closely knit staff and myself. I felt their sincere love as I read their expressions of appreciation:

"With utmost respect and appreciation."

"We'll miss you terribly; I've learned more from you than any person in my life—in every way—academically and spiritually. Everything you handle is like a velvet touch."

"Whenever I'm around you, I'm around Jesus! He constantly uplifts, encourages and strengthens through you."

"Consciously and subconsciously, one of my chief aims has been to become more like you. Howard had seminary and I had you. I have carefully watched you in joyous or troubling circumstances, in times of seeking truth and in giving answers. And always I saw God. Yosemite shows God's creative powers but you show of God's personhood and love in action."

What humbling tributes!

Finally, on the morning of June 24th, with some last minute packing of every inch of available space in the trunk of our '72 Skylark and with more painful farewells to my precious aging mother and dear sister and family, Beverly and I were on our way to Florida—to an unknown assignment and undetermined address. I felt somewhat akin to Abraham, who went out in obedience to God not really knowing where he was going. But there is such pure joy in obedience and since God has promised that the willing and obedient shall eat of the good of the land, we had nothing to fear (Isaiah 1:19). We were promised the traveling companion of the Holy Spirit of whom it is written, "He will tell you where to go and what to do..." (Galatians 5:16).

God Recycles **Broken** *Dreams*

As we headed northward through California along the magnificent Redwood Highway—walking in and driving through these giant redwoods that had stood for years—we were reminded of the greatness of our God. Surely he was capable of caring for us! As we journeyed through beautiful Oregon and then picturesque Washington, we were reminded repeatedly of the beauty and variety of God's creation. We enjoyed a ferry ride over Puget Sound to Bremerton and also a tour of the Boeing Jet Plant at Everett, Washington. The journey through British Columbia was spectacular with its exquisite Butchart Gardens (we saw how a devastated limestone quarry was transformed into a gorgeous garden), and then along the indescribable majestic canyons, mountains with their gurgling streams and cascading waterfalls and serene lakes. What an awe-inspiring experience!

But this pleasurable journey came to a screeching halt on July 1st—on a desolate stretch in the Province of Saskatchewan, Canada—when Bev over-steered and went over an embankment. In the split seconds of envisioning smashed car and broken bodies, I cried out, "Lord! Lord!" That's all I had time to say, but that's all that was necessary, for he truly was Lord of that situation, and he averted a fatal accident. How we got back on the road is covered in a previous chapter.

This frightening episode was just one of a string of events that illustrated to me Satan's opposition and even desire to kill us while we were traveling on the path of obedience to God. Didn't that arch enemy of God scheme in devious ways to destroy Jesus Christ while on his earthly mission—from early infancy when Herod decreed all male babies be destroyed, through his public ministry when angered religious leaders sought his life, right up to his crucifixion when Satan probably celebrated with his cohorts on a job well done—only to be completely shattered three days later by the bodily resurrection of our Lord? Since he is conqueror, we can be triumphant through him (II Corinthians 2:14).

Our primary reason for traveling through Canada, besides desiring to enjoy its beauty, was to visit friends who were serving on a remote Indian mission in Red Lake, Ontario. What a happy reunion that was with our Mennonite friends, Norman and Susie Stauffer with daughter Mary Elaine, formerly from Lancaster County, Pennsylvania. They welcomed us with a delicious dinner of moose meat loaf, sugar peas, potatoes, and of course, home-made bread with home-made raspberry preserves. Their five-year-old adopted Indian daughter, Stephanie, won our hearts, along with other beautiful Indian babies and children being cared for in the orphanage there. Having left a lucrative job in Pennsylvania and now giving unending hours of labor in this remote part of Canada without any financial remuneration, it was inspiring to hear Norman say, "We've never been happier!"

It was great to get back into good ole USA, and just in time for its 4th of July celebration. We had just crossed over into Minnesota and were traveling over a rather desolate part of Michigan, enroute to my brother Marvin's home in Wisconsin, when I noticed Bev, who was driving at the time, had become strangely silent. Taking a second look, I observed that she had turned very pale. "Bev, is something wrong?" I asked.

Grimacing and with tears in her eyes, she replied, "I don't know what's wrong."

Suggesting she let me drive, I became increasingly concerned for I could see her pain was becoming more acute. Pulling to a stop, I quickly scanned the map to see where the nearest town might be, and much to my dismay, it looked like we were about two hours from the nearest one. Those two hours seemed interminable as Bev suffered and I prayed—silently and aloud. I recall having heard a good suggestion in handling fears—think of the very worst thing that could happen in that particular situation and release that possibility to God. Already I had the haunting fear confront me, "What if this is an attack of acute appendicitis?" I found the next thought much more difficult to handle, "What if Bev should die before I could get her medical help?"

 God Recycles Broken Dreams

With an act of my will, I released even the worst possibility to God, realizing we were in his care and love, and then a great sense of relief came over me. Finally as we entered the outskirts of the small town of Ironwood, Michigan, we inquired as to the nearest hospital, and shortly Bev was in competent kind hands. The lab tests cancelled the probability of appendicitis, but they were unable to establish clearly the cause of this extreme pain. She was given some medication, and with the pain having subsided considerably, we resumed our journey. I was reminded of the words of the hymn, "Through many dangers, toils and snares, I have already come; 'Tis grace has brought me safe thus far, and grace will lead me home."

After a delightful time together with Marv and Grace, and Bev had become acquainted with her three growing cousins, Jay, Ricky, and Jim, we headed southward. As we traveled, we found ourselves enclosed in an exhausting heat wave with temperatures hovering around 100 degrees almost every day. Periodically, even our car air-conditioner seemed just too overworked and took some temporary respites. We especially were conscious of this intense heat wave during an unexpected eight-day delay in Roanoke, Virginia, where a car part—weakened by our accident in Canada—broke, and a replacement could not be located for over a week! Our garage man even called the Buick company in Michigan, and they did not stock that part. After numerous junkyards were contacted, finally the needed part was located. Even though this unplanned delay was quite a stressful trial, yet God was good to us in the midst of it by allowing us to be close to the Hightowers, friends of former years from my home church in Schenectady, NY, and they gave us that wonderful "make-yourself-at-home" treatment. Also, while in that area, God ministered new hope and courage to a fine couple for whose wedding I had played many years previously. In the intervening years, they had gotten discouraged and disenchanted with the ministry. So again, God used our problems to bless us and others.

Finally, after nearly four weeks of traveling 7,000 miles, we entered the state of Florida! Realizing our vacation was now over brought a more serious tone to our devotions that morning as we were in our St. Augustine motel. But the Holy Spirit illuminated an appropriate directive for me from Acts 9:6, "Now get up and go into the city and await my further instruction," and Psalm 14:5, "God is with those who love Him." So heading down toward the Orlando area, we came to Zellwood—quite unimpressive, we thought, although it was heartening to see a large billboard along the highway featuring a picture of Dr. Robert Schuller with information concerning the new church to be built there in the future.

When we entered Apopka, our hearts really sank—"God, did you call us to come all the way from California to this?" To accentuate my let-down feelings, I was aware of more car trouble. Having skipped lunch, we decided we had better get something to eat first and then locate a mechanic to work on our car. Driving slowly through town, we caught sight of a sign outside a drugstore advertising a buffeteria which appealed to us—especially after having had so many hamburger pickups enroute. Once inside, we just could not believe our eyes... there were boxes and bottles and every imaginable commodity stacked from floor to ceiling; we could hardly make our way through the aisles to the lunch area! Between gulps of food I was swallowing tears, "Lord, is this *really* where you want us?" I questioned in disbelief.

Locating a garage nearby, I was somewhat consoled to observe the name of my brother "Marv" on the mechanic's shirt—giving me a fleeting feeling of familiarity amidst all this strangeness. After a brief inspection of our car, Marv diagnosed the problem as being worn shocks besides the need for replacement of the fan belts. In the midst of all this, another lady customer stood observing our dilemma. She was God's right person... at the right place and... just the right time.

God Recycles **Broken** *Dreams*

June Goff had been busily preparing dinner in their home in Apopka when the phone rang informing her that her son's truck was ready to be picked up at this same garage that I had ventured into. Noting our California license tag and a Christian bumper sticker, "Christians aren't Perfect… Just Forgiven," she approached me with, "What brings you from California to Apopka, Florida?"

(By this time, I truly wondered, too!) I explained briefly my errand in obedience to God's call of coming to be a part of the new church at Zellwood (just north of Apopka). We seemed like long lost friends within minutes. As we started to leave, June questioned where we planned to spend the night and I pointed to a nearby motel. She followed us there in her car, but to our disappointment, there was a notice on the motel office door, "Closed for vacation." As June drove up beside us, she offered, "We don't have a fancy home, and no air-conditioning (it was an oppressively hot, humid day), but you would be so welcome to stay with us." We accepted gratefully.

So that's what the scriptural directive had meant earlier that same morning… that if I would go into the city (Apopka), I would be given further instructions. All this had come about through our unwanted car trouble—how often God leads us through and in the midst of troubles. The other side of that story is that June had prayed very earnestly just that week, "Lord, I wish I had a Christian friend that I could call anytime as a prayer partner."

"Sure didn't expect the Lord to send me one all the way from California," is what June shared with me later in astonishment—and we truly did become close friends in Christ.

Howard and June and their sons gave us a warm welcome to stay with them until we found a place of our own; what a wonderful feeling it was after searching eight to ten hours a day for a suitable place to live to know we had a delicious home-cooked meal and friendly faces and voices waiting to greet us. I must confess our feelings took some heavy slumps during that exhausting search for a place of our own, but fortunately when Bev was down, I was up… and, like a teeter-totter, when I was down, she would recite my words back to me: "Mom, it's going to work out all right… it just takes patience!"

Actually, within three days into our search, the Lord very wonderfully led us to the right mobile park, the right home, and even to a choice lot. As we were driving to the Chalet North Park, June said, "It's just all going to be so easy when it's the right place."

That is exactly how it was, even though we had tried three times earlier that morning to locate Chalet North and always had been misled. When we finally arrived, both Bev and I felt so relaxed and contented—just like we had arrived home. Isn't God good! Then when we were shown the lovely, used mobile home, with very nice homey furniture, I could not believe my eyes to see hanging on the living room wall a small picture of an identical larger picture I had very reluctantly sold before leaving California—one of Paul Detlefsen's restful barn scenes. "Oh, thank you, Lord, for giving me such a beautiful token of your approval!"

We learned that a fine Christian school teacher had been praying for the sale of this lovely home, which belonged to her elderly parents. Our prayers obviously met! As we drove around in the park, we spotted a choice corner lot with seven orange trees on it and facing a beautiful private wooded area; for a very reasonable fee, the manager agreed to move our home to that lot. So within one week we had the keys to our "new" home in Florida! "Thank you, Father!"

Being in God's will does not guarantee smooth sailing. In fact, quite often, it is to the contrary. Didn't the disciples encounter the stormy Sea of Galilee even though Christ was right in the boat with them, and didn't Paul find himself shipwrecked? For the next three months there seemed to be an ongoing "stormy weather" pattern for us—there was the hassle of waiting 35 days for our van with household goods to arrive; we had been promised it would arrive within seven days after being notified of our address. Then

God Recycles **Broken** *Dreams*

when the van finally arrived, my most valuable carton containing irreplaceable farewell gifts was missing. It arrived seven months later! It was a test of faith, and yet a miracle of God's love.

I had on-going hassles with a transfer of insurance companies including computer errors, and an IRS audit with all my receipts still on that delayed van. In the midst of trying to get settled, I suffered extreme circulatory pains which involved exorbitant medical expenses. Then we learned of the death of my former mother-in-law, our beloved Mother Shank. My brother Sam underwent a critical brain surgery in Boston, and the next month I received a phone call from California saying our precious mother had left her earthly abode to be with Jesus her Lord.

Yes, all these sorrows, losses, and hassles in my Year of Jubilee. But life is not all a fanfare or "blowing of the trumpets." There are the taps and somber tones, too... shadows as well as sunshine... bittersweet. So what was so special about my 50th year? I experienced God's amazing divine leadership at every bend in the road.

I know his hand will continue to guide me to ever-widening paths of fruitfulness for his glory.

Chapter 15
BST 4 LST

A s life goes on, God's mercies continue to abound. "O, give thanks unto the Lord for he is good; his mercies endure forever" (Psalm 136:1).

From 1977 to 1981, I was an active member of the Rolling Hills Community Church of Zellwood, Florida. I served on the steering and building committees, as well as as an elder and vice president of the consistory, the organist, and the Christian education director. It was both exciting and exhausting to be such an active participant in this beautiful new daughter church of Dr. Robert Schuller of Garden Grove, California. People came from everywhere to join this growing, friendly church nestled in an orange grove among the rolling hills of central Florida.

The founding pastor, Harold De Roo, together with his devoted wife, Dorothy, gave enthusiastic and creative leadership. His sermons were weekly wonders. He initiated the annual Easter sunrise service at the nearby Fountain Lake in the mode of a Galilean service (with the pastor coming across the lake in a boat). And the Christmas Eve celebrations in the barn with live animals and a real baby sleeping (or crying) in the hay were unforgettable experiences.

To fuse together a congregation coming from varying denominations and locales with differing traditions was at times a stressful challenge; but by God's Spirit, we gradually grew into a family of God with deep and caring love for one another.

Many of us had difficulty obtaining employment in this new setting. But by God's grace, I was hired to serve as secretary in the Marketing and Sales Department of a prestigious citrus company. Four bosses kept my fingers hopping on the typewriter—besides many other responsibilities.

At times I felt somewhat out of place in this competitive, pressurized business world. But I was reminded repeatedly by the Holy Spirit that I was exactly where God had placed me and that I was to bloom where I had been planted. (And that I might even be "scent" there)! There were innumerable opportunities to speak a word of encouragement to my fellow employees, to put a bit of pertinent wisdom on the bulletin board (since I was chairman of the board), such as "Success comes in cans... not in cannots," or to be a compassionate listener during lunch time to a heavy-hearted employee struggling with family problems.

It was a most rewarding encouragement to observe some remarkable changes in people as a result of persistent prayer. One of the executives remarked to me one day, "Ruth, I'm sure glad we have someone like you on the phone to absorb some of the frustrations of brokers and customers." Truly, there are many opportunities to share the love of Christ in the marketplace.

In the summer of 1981, I had a life-long dream fulfilled of being able to join a tour group which took us to Holland, Germany, Austria, Switzerland, Belgium and France. I was especially thrilled to be in Germany—my parents' Vaterland. And the crowning joy was to spend several days with my 83-year-old Tante Hildegard, my mother's only sister who had suffered many losses under the Nazi regime. She was a godly woman, still fruitful in her older years conducting Bible retreats for women. Somehow we felt an almost instant mother-daughter sense of kinship; we seemed to think and respond alike in so many matters, and yet we had never met until that moment.

It was about this time that I had a growing conviction that my assignment in Florida was coming to a close. God had specifically sent me there to help

God Recycles **Broken** *Dreams*

lay the foundation stones for a new church; but now after four years of work, sweat and joys, there were many capable church builders who could serve well as my replacement.

So, with mission accomplished, "Where do you need me next?" I inquired of my Commander-in-Chief. I found the older one grows, the more stressful change can be. Even the process of seeking to know God's will was grueling. I wrote countless letters, mailed out resumés and made telephone calls to various Christian organizations and colleges.

Realizing the need of inner quietness to hear the voice of God—to "Be still and know that I am God..." (Psalm 46:10a), I designated a whole Saturday to be spent at my favorite spot in Florida—Clearwater Beach. Having read Isaiah 41:1a, "Keep silence before me..." before starting on my journey, I arrived at the beautiful Gulf waters at about 9:00 a.m. Only a few beach-combers and seagulls accentuated the swishing sound of the gentle waves. It was an ideal setting to read the Scriptures and meditate.

But after five hours of this, I became restless, and almost accusingly I pouted, "Lord, you instructed me this morning through your Word to listen in silence before you. Well, that's what I've been doing for five hours, and you haven't told me a thing!"

Within ten minutes, God responded in the most unexpected fashion (doesn't he always!). Hearing a plane overhead, I glanced up to see it flying over the water dragging an advertisement behind it. These are common occurrences over the Florida beaches. But usually such advertising was for an air show, a cocktail special, and the like. But as I studied this message, I could scarcely believe my eyes, for it read: "God's number is Jeremiah 33:3. Call him today."

Fortunately, I knew that number and its message: "Call unto me, and I will answer thee, and show thee great and mighty things which thou knowest not."

I almost rolled over in the sand with holy laughter. Just to think that moments before I had accused God of not telling me anything, and now he writes a message via airmail for my benefit. How marvelous are his ways!

This remarkable evidence of God's love gave me the confidence to submit to my bosses the following Monday morning my two-weeks' notice of resigning my position. They seemed both surprised and concerned that I would take this step without another job in sight.

Through a month-long process of asking, seeking and knocking, the Lord very clearly led me to beautiful Charlottesville, Virginia to work in a unique ministry—Christian Aid Mission. This missionary organization had been pioneered by Dr. Bob Finley many years ago as a channel of encouragement and support to our indigenous brethren laboring overseas in areas of poverty and persecution. So this was indeed the fulfillment of the "… great and mighty things which thou knowest not," the message I had received at Clearwater Beach, Florida.

One Sunday evening in March 1983, I received a shocking telephone call from a hospital in Orlando, Florida advising me that my daughter, Beverly Sue, had been involved in a serious accident. The driver of a pick-up truck loaded with cement blocks had lost control, fishtailed across a road and thrown Beverly off of her bicycle into a wild bushy area. It was learned that the driver had been drinking and was driving without a license.

My first reaction was shock and an outpouring of tears. Immediately, though, I thanked God that her life had been spared. In the intervening anxious hours until I was able to arrive at her bedside in the intensive care unit, I claimed Romans 8:28 (KJV), "And we know that all things work together for good to them that love God, to them who are called according to his purpose." And in the process of weeks and months to follow, we saw God transform a traumatic nightmare into beautiful blessings.

God Recycles **Broken** *Dreams*

After Bev's recovery, she moved to Virginia to complete her college education, and in the spring of 1985 she graduated with a BS degree in Biology. She then worked in the Biochem Lab at the University of Virginia in Charlottesville.

My Virginia state license tag bears the message, BST 4 LST, which expresses my true hope and dreams. And truly the Lord has been fulfilling those dreams in remarkable ways. Having lived in the beautiful state of Virginia for six years, I wished for a small home of my own with a big view. After several weeks of intensive searching, I learned of a spacious wooded area with a spectacular mountain view being developed into home lots. The Lord had promised, "My people shall dwell in a peaceable habitation, and in sure dwellings, and in quiet resting places" (Isaiah 32:18 KJV).

My spirit sensed this was the right place while my mind questioned how Beverly and I could manage the financial transaction. Within a few days, God marvelously provided a generous down payment from an unexpected source. How thrilled and grateful we were! It was so exciting to watch our dream home being built during the next several months. In October of 1987, we were given the key to our adorable 1500-square-foot home.

Beverly suggested that if I would take care of decorating the inside of our home, she would be responsible to beautify the outside—a fair deal for me. Our yard abounds with hundreds of flowers, shrubs and trees, while I have had the pleasure of arranging a cozy, inviting interior.

After settling into our new nest, as I would take frequent walks, I mentioned to the Lord how nice it would be to have another "bird" join the nest to make it complete. The Lord took note of that request in a startling fashion. One summer evening in June 1988, while I was sitting on our backyard adult swing set enjoying the colorful sunset and meditating on the goodness of God, suddenly I became aware of an inner voice announcing, "You will have a husband by the end of this year."

Before I was even able to respond, the exact same message was repeated two more times. By then I knew it was God speaking to me. With tear-filled eyes, I responded, "I only ask that he would love you and love me and that our lives together would be more effective for your Kingdom than separately." What a sacred scene! Too sacred to share with any human being—not even my daughter who was my best friend.

June... July... August... September—all came and went without any new developments. But I was not anxious. I knew God had promised and he would provide. Finally, on the first Sunday evening of October, the telephone rang. It was my older sister, Violet, calling from California. "Ruthie, how would you like a nice husband?" She queried.

Although my heart was racing, I responded in a nonchalant tone, "Perhaps, who is he?"

As soon as I had hung up the receiver, I fell on my knees at my bedside and prayed, "Lord, is this the one you told me about back in June?"

And his immediate reply was, "Every good gift and every perfect gift is from above, and cometh down from the Father of lights, with whom is no variableness, neither shadow of turning" (James 1:17 KJV).

I had perfect peace and fullness of joy.

My sister had met my husband-to-be, Gordon Shira, a retired Lutheran minister, while offering Spanish lessons to him and others involved in a missionary outreach in Mexico.

In I Samuel 21:8 (KJV), we are told, "The King's business requires haste." And so it was with our courtship. Through an amazingly short period of intense correspondence, phone calls, and finally a visit by Gordon to Charlottesville, we knew God had indeed arranged a holy love affair. It culminated in a lovely wedding attended by one hundred friends on December 17, 1988. I had even purchased my wedding dress before I actually met

God Recycles **Broken** *Dreams*

Gordon because I was so sure of God's promise. We enjoyed a honeymoon in Colonial Williamsburg.

Of course, there were adjustments since each of us had lived alone for about 20 years, but knowing God had brought us together for his purposes kept us on track. Also, there were stressful times when Gordon faced surgery for prostate cancer and when Beverly became victim of a chronic illness. Beginning and ending each day together with Bible reading and prayer kept us strong in the Lord.

Gordon has been a unique gift of God to me now for nearly 25 years. He is a godly gentleman with a giving heart who "walks out" the word of God in daily living. Gordon would not tell you how God used him almost miraculously in pastoring Lutheran mission churches in Indiana and Illinois. One church grew from 34 (counting pregnant women twice) to over 800. The other one exploded to over 1200 attendants.

He also pastored two churches in California. While located in the Los Angeles area, he ministered in five missions on "Skid Row," where it was estimated 30,000 homeless people barely existed. Gordon was best known as the "socks preacher" because he distributed thousands of pairs of socks to the homeless in areas where nights are surprisingly cold.

Gordon had often desired to pastor a church without receiving a salary, and this happened in his last pastorate in California. For a means of income, he was hired by the LA Department of Parks and Recreation to oversee the programs for senior citizens. As Director of one of the senior centers with 2500 seniors, he arranged tours and a variety of activities together with refreshments five days a week. After 10 years Gordon retired receiving high accolades for having made such a difference in the lives of seniors.

When he came to Virginia, Gordon was soon involved with the ministry of Christian Aid for four years. He also served as chaplain for the local Salvation Army for 14 years, and for the past 20 years, he has served at Advancing Native Missions in the receipting department and also as their chaplain.

The foundation of ANM is in Matthew 24:14 (NLT), "And the Gospel will be preached throughout the world, so that all nations will hear it, and then, finally, the end will come." Rather than sending missionaries from North America to evangelize these areas of the world, ANM seeks out capable, godly indigenous leaders who already know the language and understand the culture, and thereby can communicate the Gospel most effectively to their own people.

So, at age 87, Gordon drives 50 miles round trip to the ANM headquarters three days a week. He often says that this is the most glorious privilege he has had in serving the Lord of the Harvest in all of his 60 years of ministry. I remind him that he has not retired, but rather has been "refired."

Besides Gordon being such a blessing to me personally and to ANM, he has been a tremendous blessing to my daughter, Beverly, who has been chronically ill for over 20 years. He has been a godly father image to her—something lacking in her life since she was 8 years old.

I'll close with an incredible story of how God used Gordon to help restore my first husband, Lloyd. He had been deeply hurt by religious legalism, and consequently had "thrown in the towel" not only to the ministry but also to our 20-year marriage. What really intensified my distraught heart was that instead of fellow believers endeavoring to restore him, they took the role of accusing critics—whether silently or verbally. I witnessed what I had heard, that "Only the Lord's army shoots its wounded soldiers."

But the Lord had not forsaken me. In fact, the faithful Holy Spirit highlighted a rather obscure scripture which comforted me because it revealed God's unfailing love. "A bruised reed he will not break, and a smoldering wick he will not snuff out" (Isaiah 42:3 NIV).

God Recycles **Broken** *Dreams*

Although Gordon had never met Lloyd personally, yet frequently when Lloyd called Beverly by phone from Florida where he was living, since she was unable to respond because of her illness, the two men engaged in conversation. Over a period of time, as Gordon developed a friendship with Lloyd reminding him of all the positive blessings of his pastoral work, gradually the Holy Spirit rekindled the flame of love for God's Kingdom in his heart.

What a beautiful, peaceful closure both for me and Beverly when the Lord called his servant Lloyd home several years ago.

So, thank you, dear heavenly Father, precious Lord Jesus Christ and ever-present Holy Spirit for not only being ever present with us on our earthly journey, but also for "Recycling Broken Dreams."

In conclusion, allow me to brag on God's marvelous recycling process by sharing a poem he gave to me in 1988.

My Two Sons

In the year of 1951
A precious son was born to me;
But without life or breath—
What a tragedy!

For many years the Lord had promised
Sons would come from afar;
I'd often wonder and ponder—
Even bringing daughters on their arms.

He also promised I'd look and be radiant.
My heart would throb and swell with joy
Because of the riches brought my way
From nations of their employ.

These treasures of God
Arrived one by one;
First, Bo Barredo from the Philippines,
Then P.R. Misra of India—two wonderful sons!

How can I fully describe
These precious sons—Bo and P.R.?
It would require volumes
To tell of their work, both here and afar.

Bo, a brilliant attorney,
But also a humble servant of the Lord;
A model gentleman, compassionate and kind
Always ready to assimilate and practice the Word.

P.R., so articulate and poised.
Full of enthusiasm and fun;
Yet takes seriously God's assignments
And from problems will never run.

Without their precious wives,
These sons are incomplete;
Anju, a princess bride,
And Marlou so charming and sweet.

So, dear sons and daughters,
You are forever in my heart;
God's love has planted you there
Never to depart.

God Recycles **Broken** *Dreams*

And, I'm reminded once again
That God never deals in less;
Instead of *one* son I had hoped for
With *two* I have been blessed.

by Ruth Shira, 1988

To God be all the glory. No wonder my personalized Virginia license tag bore the message, "BST 4 LST!" And the very best is yet to come when all earthly sorrows will be forgotten, and all tears will be wiped away in the presence of our glorious Redeemer.

Epilogue

Someone once said, "Old age comes at such a bad time." Perhaps in some ways, but I have learned, with the help of the Holy Spirit, some more uplifting perspectives.

In the midst of your own challenges, think and pray for others who are in an even more difficult situation than yours.

Don't nurse regrets of the past. Remember our determined enemy—Satan—is an "accuser of the brethren—"(Rev. 12:10 KJV). However, "Greater is he that is in you than he that is in the world" (I John 4:4b KJV).

Instead of dwelling on the things you are no longer able to do, be thankful for what you can do now, by God's grace, in this season of your life. There are ages and stages, and you can still be fruitful in your older years. "Even in old age they will still produce fruit; they will remain vital and green" (Psalm 92:14 NLT).

Remind yourself frequently that you are not a citizen of this troublesome world; you are just passing through enroute to your glorious eternal home in Heaven.

Charles Spurgeon made this remarkable statement, "The best moment of a Christian's life is his last one because that is nearest Heaven."

We do not have to fear death because our Savior has already defeated our last enemy through his victorious resurrection.

"Death means the sleep of the body,

And who's afraid to sleep?

Death means to be present with the Lord,

And who's afraid to be present with the Lord?

Death means to be at home with God,

And who's afraid to go home?" (Anonymous)

I trust the following scenario will be true at the end of your earthly journey:

"When you were born, you cried while the whole world rejoiced.

Live your life in such a manner that when you die, the whole world cries while you rejoice." (Anonymous)

A GOLDEN PROMISE FOR OUR GOLDEN YEARS

"I created you and have cared for you since before you were born. I will be your God throughout your lifetime, until your hair is white with age. I made you, and I will care for you. I will carry you along and sustain you" (Isaiah 46:3b-4 NLT).

God Recycles **Broken** *Dreams*

About the Author

Born in Stuyvesant Falls, New York, Ruth Shira has lived in seven different states.

She received her B.Rel.Ed. from United Wesleyan College in Allentown, Pennsylvania and her M.Ed. from Florida Atlantic University.

She served as pastoral assistant in charge of music, as well as serving children's and women's ministries in several churches where her husband was pastor.

Mrs. Shira was also involved in public school teaching in several states and served as principal in a private Christian school in California.

Having lived in Virginia for the past 32 years, she has been active in indigenous missionary outreach—first at Christian Aid Mission, and since 1992 at Advancing Native Missions which serves as an advocate for 5000 indigenous missionaries in 80 countries. Ruth and her husband, Gordon Shira, are known affectionately as "Mom and Dad" at ANM.

Ruth's desire to share her testimony and purpose for writing this book is best expressed in Psalm 71:17-18 (NLT): "O God, you have taught me from my earliest childhood, and I have constantly told others about the wonderful things you do. Now that I am old and gray, do not abandon me, O Lord. Let me proclaim your power to the next generation, your mighty miracles to all who come after me."

The Ministry of ANM

ANM Publications is a ministry initiative of Advancing Native Missions

Advancing Native Missions (ANM) is a U.S.-based Christian missions agency. However, unlike many such agencies that are involved in sending missionaries from America to other places around the world, ANM works with indigenous missionaries. Indigenous (or native) missionaries are Christian workers who minister within their own sphere of influence proclaiming the Gospel of Jesus Christ to their own people. ANM then works to connect Christians in America with these brothers and sisters, to equip and encourage them.

Our goal is to build relationships of love and trust between indigenous missionaries and North American individuals and churches. In this way, the entire body of Christ becomes involved in completing the Great Commission. **"And this gospel of the kingdom shall be preached in all the world as a witness to all nations, and then the end shall come"** (Matthew 24:14).

If you would like to know how you can become an effective coworker with native missionaries to reach the unreached for Jesus Christ, contact ANM at requests@adnamis.org, call us at 540-456-7111, or visit our website:

www.AdvancingNativeMissions.com

CPSIA information can be obtained at www.ICGtesting.com
Printed in the USA
BVOW08s1906200216

437472BV00001B/17/P